THE CENTRE CANNOT HOLD

THE CENTRE CANNOT HOLD

Britain's Failure in Northern Ireland

TOM COLLINS

With a Foreword by
the Nobel Peace Laureate
SEÁN MacBRIDE

Bookworks Ireland
Dublin • Belfast

EPIGRAPH

The Athenians, who were at war with Sparta, wanted to force the inhabitants of the little island of Melos, allied to Sparta from all antiquity and so far remaining neutral, to join with them. It was in vain that the men of Melos, faced with the ultimatum of the Athenians, invoked justice, imploring pity for the antiquity of their town. As they would not give in, the Athenians razed their city to the ground, put all their men to death and sold all their women and children as slaves.

Thucydides has put the lines in question into the mouth of these Athenians. They begin by saying that they will not try to prove that their ultimatum is just.

"Let us treat rather of what is possible. . . . You know it as well as we do; the human spirit is so constituted that what is just is only examined if there is equal necessity on both sides. But if one is strong and the other weak, that which is possible is imposed by the first and accepted by the second."

The men of Melos said that in the case of a battle they would have the gods with them on account of the justice of their cause. The Athenians replied that they saw no reason to suppose so.

"As touching the gods we have the belief, and as touching men the certainty, that always by a necessity of nature, each one commands wherever he has the power. We did not establish this law, we are not the first to apply it; we found it already established, we abide by it as something likely to endure forever; and that is why we apply it. We know quite well that you also, like all the others, once you reached the same degree of power, would act in the same way."

Simone Weil

Cover: British soldier removing gelignite bomb from the Irish Kitchen of The Melville Hotel on Foyle Street, Derry, 1972.

SEÁN MacBRIDE, winner of the Nobel Prize for Peace in 1974, is a former Foreign Minister of the Republic of Ireland; a co-founder of Amnesty International; a Signatory to the Geneva Conventions of 1949; a Signatory to the European Convention for the Promotion of Human Rights (1950). He was Secretary General of the International Commission of Jurists (1963-1971), Assistant Secretary-General of the United Nations and UN Commissioner for Namibia (1973-1976). He was awarded the Lenin Peace Prize in 1977; the American Medal of Justice in 1978; the Award of the International Institute of Human Rights in 1978; and the Order of the Pike of the Ancient Order of Hibernians in America in 1978.

First published
1983 by
BOOKWORKS IRELAND
27 Bayside Park
Dublin 13

Made and printed in Ireland
ISBN 0 8298 0631 8

PHOTO CREDITS

Except where indicated, photographs are the property of PACEMAKER PRESS INTERNATIONAL LTD. Other photographers and photographic sources:

AP/Wide World 103. Larry Doherty cover, 10-11, 25, 50-51, 57, 70-71, 73, 87, 91 top. Barney McMonagle 54-55, 60-61, 69, 76-77, 97. The Irish Press 111, 138-139, 165. The Irish Times 44-45, 93. Press Association 34. The Times 39, 90, 144. Unidentified 82. UPI/Popperfoto 62, 88, 107.

ACKNOWLEDGEMENTS

Virtually all the sources from which excerpts herein are taken are protected by copyright, and materials from them may not be reproduced in any form without the consent of the authors or their publishers or agents. Every effort has been made to trace the ownership of all excerpts used in this book and to obtain the necessary authorization for their use. If any errors or omissions have occurred in this regard, corrections will be made in all future editions of the book.

Anthony Wedgwood Benn, selection from BBC radio interview 12 May 1981.

Alun Chalfont, selection from "The Balance of Military Forces" in *The Ulster Debate*, The Bodley Head, Ltd., London; copyright © 1972 by Alun Chalfont and The Bodley Head.

Claud Cockburn, selections from *The Irish Times* (Dublin), 2/9/81, 12/8/81; copyright © 1981 by *The Irish Times*.

Tim Pat Coogan, selection from *The I.R.A.*, Fontana Books: William Collins Sons & Co., Ltd., London; copyright © 1970, 1980 by Timothy Patrick Coogan.

James Craig (Lord Craigavon), selection from a speech made 24 April 1934.

Maurice Craig selection from his "Ballad to a Traditional Refrain," copyright c 1983 by Maurice Craig.

Samuel Dash, selection from *Justice Denied*, NCCL, London, 1973; copyright © 1973 by Samuel Dash.

Liam de Paor, selections from *Divided Ulster*, Penguin Books, Ltd., Harmondsworth, England; copyright © 1971 by Liam de Paor.

Bernadette Devlin, selection from *The Price of My Soul*, Pan Books, Ltd., London; copyright © 1969 by Bernadette Devlin.

T.S. Eliot, selections from "The Waste Land" (Part 1, "The Burial of the Dead") in *Collected Poems 1909-1962*, Faber and Faber, Ltd., London; copyright © 1963 by T.S. Eliot.

Denis Faul and Raymond Murray, British Army and RUC Special Branch Brutalities: 1971-72, Abbey Printers, Cavan; copyright © 1972 by Denis Faul and Raymond Murray.

Fortnight editorial from *Fortnight: An Independent Review for Northern Ireland* (Belfast), issue No. 160 (1978); cover of issue No. 195 (1983). Used by permission.

Grattan Freyer, review in *Books Ireland* (Goslingstown, Kilkenny, Ireland). September 1981; copyright © 1981 by *Books Ireland*.

Graham Greene, selection from letter to *The Times* (London), 26/11/71.

John Hume, selection from article "The Irish Question: A British Problem" in *The Irish Times* (Dublin), 21/5/80; copyright © 1980 by *The Irish Times*.

Thomas Kinsella, selections from "Butcher's Dozen: A Lesson for the Octave of Widgery" in *Fifteen Dead*, The Dolmen Press, Portlaoise, Ireland; copyright © 1972, 1979 by Thomas Kinsella.

Brigadier Frank Kitson, selection from *Low-Intensity Operations: Subversion, Insurgency, Peacekeeping*, Faber and Faber, London; copyright © 1971 by Frank Kitson.

Clive Limpkin, selection from *The Battle of Bogside*, Penguin Books, Ltd., Harmondsworth, England; copyright © 1972 by Clive Limpkin.

Thomas Madden account from *Political Murder in Northern Ireland* by Martin Dillon and Denis Lehane, Penguin Books, Ltd., Harmondsworth, England; copyright © 1973 by Martin Dillon and Denis Lehane.

Maria Maguire, selection from *To Take Arms: A Year in the Provisional IRA*, Macmillan & Company, Ltd, London; copyright © 1973 by Maria Maguire.

Eamonn McCann, selections from *War and an Irish Town*, Pluto Press Limited, London; copyright © 1974, 1980 by Eamonn McCann.

Mahood *Daily Mail* cartoon: Tuesday 27 September 1983. Used by permission.

David W. Miller, selection from *The Queen's Rebels*, Gill and Macmillan, Dublin; copyright © 1972 by David W. Miller.

Jan Morris, selection from "A Welsh View of Ireland" in *The New York Times*, 11/6/81; copyright © 1982 by *The New York Times*.

Terence O'Neill, selection from broadcast in May 1969.

George Bernard Shaw, selections from *The Matter with Ireland*, Hart-Davis, London, 1962; and from speech made December 1912 in the Memorial Hall, London.

A.T.Q. Stewart, selection from *The Narrow Ground*, Faber and Faber, London; copyright © 1977 by A.T.Q. Stewart.

Sunday Times editorial selection from *The Sunday Times* (London), 23/8/81.

Peter Taylor, selection from *Beating the Terrorists*, Penguin Books, Ltd., Harmondsworth, England; copyright © 1980 by Peter Taylor.

Andy Tyrie, selection as reported in *The Irish Times* (Dublin), 16/6/81.

Simone Weil, selection from *Waiting on God*, Fountain Books: William Collins Sons & Co., Ltd., London.

Peregrine Worsthorne, editorial selection from *The Sunday Telegraph* (London), 3/5/81.

William Butler Yeats, selections from "The Second Coming" and "The Stare's Nest By My Window." Reprinted by permission of Michael B. Yeats, Anne Yeats and Macmillan London Limited.

Contents

(Left) Image of a gunman: Northern Ireland, 1975.

(Left) Catholic woman in Derry in confrontation with RUC inspector, backed by British Army troopers, when checkpoints were set up in Derry in 1972.

Foreword

Since I ceased to be active in the Irish political scene, I have avoided dealing with Irish affairs and Anglo-Irish relationships; hence, it was with some hesitation that I agreed to write the Foreword for this book when Tom Collins approached me. I have now come to the conclusion that to maintain silence on the events that are tearing our nation apart is no longer possible. Silence would imply consent.

While I understand the motivation of the armed Republican forces that are struggling for the reunification of Ireland, I disagree with the methods which they are using. Indeed, I believe that, in this day and age, it should be possible to bring about the reunification of Ireland by peaceful and political means. It is probably the failure of our political parties, North and South, to make any serious attempt to undo partition that has prompted and encouraged the armed violence which has been escalating at an increasing tempo over the last fourteen years. Had a firmer leadership of the nationalist-Republican forces been forthcoming, the extreme policies of the IRA and other groups would not have flourished. While politicians have mentioned partition frequently, they have created the impression that this was ritualistic formality and that they really did not intend to do anything about it; they seemed to be really more interested in strengthening their own political base in the twenty-six Counties than in re-unifying the country. One may even have got the impression from time to time that they were prepared to collaborate covertly with the British Establishment in Belfast and London to ensure that no-one rocked the boat on the Partition issue.

11

This lack of leadership on the part of the political parties created the feeling of despair and abandonment that led to the hunger-strike.

Because of this ambivalence on the part of our political leaders, there has also been a tendency to minimize the nature and extent of the injustices and sufferings which the Irish people have been subjected to as a result of the settlement imposed on Ireland in 1921 under the threat of "immediate and terrible war" by the British government, causing a bitter Civil War which lasted for close on three years. Apart from the losses in terms of human lives and material damage, the Civil War created a deep and bitter division among the Irish people. Some of that bitterness still survives today, and the basic division between the two main political parties stems from the Civil War.

As far as the majority of the Irish people are concerned, while the Republicans lost the Civil War militarily in the 1920s, they won it politically with the adoption of the 1937 Constitution, and with the establishment of the Republic in 1949. However, the Civil War did distort attitudes and retard progress in the country. We were able to undo all the objectionable provisions imposed by the Anglo-Irish Treaty of 1921, save the Partition of the country. The continued Partition of the country has led to organized armed insurrection, North and South, with practically no interruption for well over half a century. The only short lull was the period between 1948-1951 when the Government in power provided an active leadership in regard to Partition. This was the only period in the course of the last sixty years in which there were no political prisoners, no executions, no hunger strikes, no special courts. Otherwise, for over sixty years our jails North and South have been bulging with politically motivated prisoners.

Time after time new internment camps, and prison camps, were built and filled. Public Safety Acts, Emergency Powers Acts, Treason Acts, Offences Against the State Acts, Law Enforcement Acts and Special Powers Acts, have succeeded each other both North and South, and have virtually destroyed the rule of law system which should prevail in any democratic state. The police forces, North and South, have been doubled, and have continually been increased by new auxiliary bodies. The Irish Army has been converted into a virtual military police force. The British Army has been drafted in substantial numbers into Northern Ireland.

Strangely enough, no one has as yet quantified the cost of Partition in terms of human lives lost in the Republic, Northern Ireland or Britain. I am sure that by now it must be something like ten thousand lives lost over the last sixty years. Nobody has attempted to evaluate the financial cost to the Republic, to Northern Ireland or to Britain of the war which has been waged incessantly since 1922 in order to maintain Partition. Added to the physical loss of lives and materiel, these events have torn apart the heart and soul of the Irish people. They have embittered relations between Ireland and England; they have affected the world at large. Strangely enough, no one in Britain or in Ireland ever seems to assess the damage that

(Above) British soldier of Scots Guards in October 1971, at Army post where a fellow guardsman was killed in an explosion the day before.

Partition has done to Ireland. These are more than unpleasant considerations. Partition is a clear-cut indication of the failure of the policies pursued over the last sixty years.

In order to avoid facing and dealing with Partition as a reality we encourage the development of a slave mentality in many areas of our national life. Our history books have become distorted, our radio and television media are not allowed to air some traditional ballads. Efforts continue to be made to subdue or curb any form of idealism or national enthusiasm.

Many will not agree with the foregoing analysis. I think all must agree, however, that the enforced Partition of our country has inflicted colossal damage to the Irish Nation — and to the British Nation as well. And it has *not worked*. It has been a costly failure.

Britain likes to place herself in the role of being the "honest broker" between two warring Irish factions. But let it not be forgotten that it was Britain that created Partition and imposed it, and that it is Britain that has supported Partition financially, militarily and politically over the last sixty years, at tremendous expense. In addition to the financial and military support extended by Britain to maintain the six county State as one of her colonies, the role of the British Secret Service, operating both in the North and in the Republic, should never be forgotten or underestimated. For every one case of covert criminal activity carried out by the British Secret Services in Ireland that comes to light, it may be assumed that there are twenty other covert criminal operations about which we are never informed.

Any powerful country can easily disrupt a small neighbouring State by means of financial and covert actions, backed by military force and an all-powerful secret service. So long as Britain continues to underwrite Partition financially, militarily and politically, and uses her secret services to carry out covert actions in the North and in the Republic, it will not be possible to end Partition. The first essential must be a cessation of all covert actions by Britain's secret services in the North and in the Republic, and a categorical renunciation of sovereignty over any portion of Ireland. As the Anglican Bishop John Austin Baker put it, when he was Chaplain to the Speaker of the British House of Commons:

> Our injustice created the situation and by constantly repeating that we will maintain it so long as the majority wish it, we actively inhibit Protestant and Catholic from working out a new future together.

The Irish Nation consists of an island comprising thirty-two counties; it is the will of the majority of Ireland's inhabitants that should be allowed to determine the future of the Irish Nation, and not the will of the inhabitants of two or even six counties.

Seán MacBride, S.C.

(Left) In Belfast, on 16 November 1975, three-year old Patricia McCullough puts down a memorial cross for the seventeen-year old brother Patrick she never knew. He had been killed three years earlier on his way home from church.

Preface

This is an attempt to show what has really been going on in Northern Ireland during the past decade and a half, and to suggest some factors which, if attended to, could bring this conflict rapidly toward resolution. It is not an intractable problem, though it serves the interests of some to insist or pretend that it is.

Few books these days are ever the work of one hand. For their help in engendering objectivity about the subject matter, I am heavily indebted to two men who for very different reasons must here be thanked anonymously. I am also indebted to the various commentators cited in and alongside the text. The political judgments and applications, however, are my own responsibility.

I am grateful especially to Seán MacBride, Ireland's most distinguished citizen, for lending his support to the book; to Mary O'Sullivan and Ruadhan Hayes for their judicious editorial assistance and to Emer Sheridan for her generous help in the preparation of the manuscript.

A special word of thanks to those like Larry Doherty who have generously contributed their photographs, and above all to Frank Carvill and Martin Wright who made the matchless archives of the Pacemaker Press International Agency available for the book. Finally, thanks with love to my wife Patricia who was the inspiration and sustaining force of this project through all the months of difficult work.

Tom Collins
Belfast
1983

Interior of the La Mon House Hotel after explosion
on 17 February 1978

Origins
of the
<u>Conflict</u>

I had not thought death
had undone so many . . .
T.S. Eliot

Belfast landscape, 1981: Lower Falls, underneath spires of St. Peter's Church, Divis.

1
A Wasted Land?

(Left top) An RUC sergeant, Cecil Haire, survivor of a booby-trap bomb explosion in Shane's Road, Andersonstown, Belfast, in April 1981, attending funeral of a colleague killed in the explosion.

(Left bottom) Jimmy McKee, a part-time member of the UDR — the Ulster Defence Regiment — killed near Omagh, Co. Tyrone, in April 1978.

(Below) The eight sisters of dead hunger striker Thomas McElwee carry his coffin from his home to the local church at Bellaghy, Co. Derry, on 10 August 1981. From left the young McElwee women are Enda, Kathleen, Nora, Annie and Majella. Also carrying the coffin are Mary, Bernadette and Pauline. At left is Magherafelt district councillor Oliver Hughes, brother of Thomas McElwee's fellow hunger striker Francis Hughes.

(Left) Nuala Lowry at the funeral of her best friend, 14-year-old Julie Livingstone, in Belfast. Nuala was present when her friend was fatally wounded by a British Army plastic bullet on 12 May, 1981. Plastic bullets were banned from use in Britain on the grounds that they were too lethal, but British authorities continued their use in Northern Ireland even after Julie Livingstone and other children had been killed, blinded or irreversibly brain-damaged by them.

(Below) Wife of RUC constable Gary Martin, killed in April 1981, at her husband's funeral.

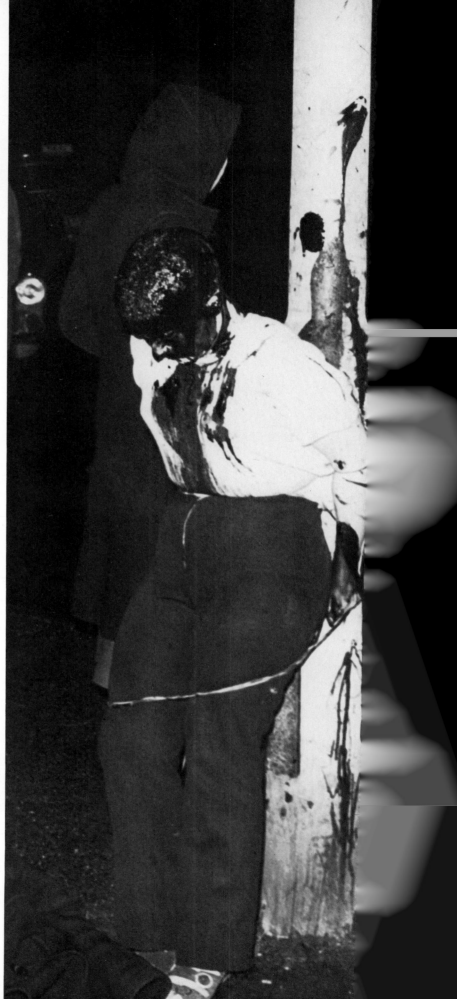

(Above and right) Marta Doherty, a Catholic girl in Derry, engaged to be married to a British soldier, tarred and tied to a post by nationalist women in July 1971.

(Left)   Paisleyite councillor calling for hanging of hunger strikers outside Maze prison at Long Kesh at time Bobby Sands was dying: late April 1981.

Boy passing burning trucks after rioting in Twin-brook, Belfast, following death of hunger striker Micky Devine in August 1981.

This war — and it is a war . . .

Seán MacBride

West Belfast in the evening (Falls Road at Grosvenor Road). Taken in 1976 from the Royal Victoria Hospital, with Cavehill Mountain on the right.

Oh the bricks they will bleed
And the rain it will weep,
And the damp Lagan fog
Lull the city to sleep;
It's to hell with the future
And live on the past:
May the Lord in His mercy
Be kind to Belfast.

Maurice Craig

(Left) Protestant workers marching to Belfast City Hall in May 1972 to protest shooting incident at Mackie's Foundry on Springfield Road in which fellow workers were injured.

2
Symbolic History

MOST COMMENTATORS like to employ Irish history to support handwringing lectures on the intractability of the Northern Ireland problem: as though an inexplicable religious fanaticism explained the conflict, or an impenetrable irrationality.

These commentators, especially when English-trained, seem to take great satisfaction in finding in the million and a half people in northeast Ireland all the dark chaotic drivings of mankind. Almost with the glee of conservators of an obscene secret, these commentators anxiously cultivate their garden of horrors, and keep watering it with their nightmare imaginings of a bloody aftermath.

Naturally they conclude from their own revulsion that the conflict must indefinitely remain unresolved.

There are, however, quite simple and unmysterious explanations for the violence and fanaticism that do exist. And the solution of the problem is clear: The wretched illness that shakes Northern Ireland can be cured by removing the cancer that sustains it.

First, though, it will be useful to run through the conflict to date, beginning with a look at the native communities and their dispute.

Historical commentators are right to this extent: there are images laden with dark emotion that appear

31

in the pre-history of the conflict, images all too readily stirred into recollection as collective signifiers of the Protestants' or Catholics' plight: richly coloured symbolic memories, derived from real and imagined historical events.

These are myths of a sort — in the sense that they are constructions in the minds and memories of the people: stories within which the antagonists shelter themselves when under attack and in terms of which they justify their actions.

They are not myths in the sense that they were predominantly false accounts which might easily be washed away from ethnic memory by enlightened — still less by secular — education.

The historical images are *not* the key to the problem. But they say a lot about the subconscious of the people on the ground in Northern Ireland.

THE PLANTATIONS. For *Northern Ireland Catholics** a sense of being outraged by England and its agents over a period of centuries was the force that through the green fuse drove the flower of antagonism. Perhaps the hardest and bitterest symbol for Catholics was that of the Ulster Plantations. In their folk memory of the Plantations, Catholics seized on features of conquest by an alien people, systematic

*"Catholics" here and afterwards means not so much the religious as what might be called the ethno/political group: the descendants of the "native" and underdog Irish. Similarly with the term "Protestants," to define the descendants of the Scottish and English "planters," topdogs in Northern Ireland who always considered themselves under threat from the other three quarters (now nearly four-fifths) of the population of the island of Ireland.

In some ways it would be better to talk of Irish "nationalists" rather than Catholics, and of "republicans" when adverting to their more vigorously nationalistic partisans; or of British "unionists" where describing the Protestant middle and upper classes, and of "loyalists" when talking about working class activists and those who are more vociferously anti-Irish-nationalist.

In truth, there are (as there have always been) Protestant nationalists. There are even Catholic unionists; in fact the one significant moderate unionist party, Alliance, takes its name from the association within it of moderate unionist Catholics with moderate unionist Protestants.

A further complication is that many in Northern Ireland, while naturally curious enough about the background of anyone they deal with, are either sick of the whole business of definition and division, or else simply don't give a damn.

Popular apathy is wildly underestimated by those who talk of a million Protestant unionists or half a million Catholic nationalists.

Many people in Northern Ireland are no more Irish nationalist or British unionist than your Jewish grandmother.

(Left) An H-Block march at Toome, Co. Antrim, in May 1981.

and violent expropriation of Catholic lands, and a bitter sense of racial pogrom: a sharp awareness of an English genocidal design — fortunately not fully followed through on by other English — a design to wipe out as far as possible the then Irish race.

Records are poor for the plantations period, but what Catholics felt was clear enough. Immediately after the death of Queen Elizabeth I, whose minions had so much trouble subduing the obdurate Irish, some of the hereditary Irish Catholic chieftains of Ulster, now earls — i.e., reduced to the status of mere English noblemen — took flight to Europe. On the suspicion that the earls were off to raise an army against their English masters — or using this supposition as an excuse — the English crown declared the earls' lands forfeit and, beginning in 1609, set out to systematically resettle their lands with English and (mainly) Scots colonists, driving those native Irish who survived off good land onto bad or into a condition of virtual serfdom.

The Ulster Protestant version of the history of the plantations begins with a picture of a vagrant and savage Irish people who had been so disloyal to their legitimate English masters that they had to be put down by force. Most of the settler people, being of stern Calvinistic stock, lived not in idolatry and superstition like the Catholic barbarians but according to a severe and self-denying biblical religion. As righteous men they thanked God for this new Israel they had been sent to make flourish, a land God had given them — a land of which they saw themselves as the first true cultivators.

THE REBELLION OF 1641 AND THE BRIDGE AT PORTADOWN. *The Protestant perception* of the "great rebellion" of 1641 and after, was of a native Catholic rising — with Anglo-Irish Catholic support — against the God-fearing settler people. The rising turned into an anti-Protestant pogrom, as for example, when men, women and children were driven onto and off the bridge at Portadown by armed Catholics and drowned, with survivors piked or shot dead.

Tales were told in England of how drunken Catholics, besotted with Romish superstition and driven by an atavistic hatred, had under the leadership of "blood-thirsty Jesuits" slaughtered some twelve thousand Protestant men, women and children, and of how these murderous Catholics used red hot tongs and gridirons to torture their victims into revealing where their money was. The Catholics raped pregnant women; they roasted infants on spits; they drove the innocent, God-fearing Protestants naked into the mountains.

(Left)   Petrol bomber in Belfast, May 1981.

To the glorious, pious and Immortal Memory
of King William III,
who saved us from Rogues and Roguery,
Slaves and Slavery,
Knaves and Knavery,
Popes and Popery,
from brass money and wooden shoes;
and whoever denies this Toast
may he be slammed, crammed and jammed
into the muzzle of the great gun of Athlone,
and the gun fired into the Pope's belly,
and the Pope into the Devil's belly,
and the Devil into Hell,
and the door locked
and the key in an Orangeman's pocket.

Orange toast
Early nineteenth century

The Catholic perception was that all this was largely untrue though based on a thin ground of fact. The numbers were exaggerated out of all proportion. The tortures were trumped up in the style of contemporary "Popish plot" literature.

CROMWELL. In 1650, in response to Catholic militancy, real and alleged, the bloody-minded Puritan Oliver Cromwell came storming along the east coast of Ireland with fire and sword, massacring everyone within reach — men, women and children. According to some accounts more than six hundred thousand Irish people perished during Cromwell's campaign, many of them by plague and famine, while a hundred thousand others were sold into slavery in the colonies.

Cromwell's slaughter was the worst evil ever visited by the English on Ireland — except for the famine two centuries later, when, during a series of potato blights, the callous British Government of the time kept exporting huge quantities of Irish-grown food to Britain and elsewhere while more than a million Irish people starved to death. There was also mass emigration, and the population of Ireland was halved.

The Protestant view of Cromwell was that he gave the rebellious Catholics the treatment they deserved. The famine was largely due to the shiftlessness of the native Irish.

THE SIEGE OF DERRY AND THE BATTLE OF THE BOYNE. *For Protestants* the founding of the Orange Order in 1795 evoked their association with William of Orange, the Dutchman to whom English Protestants had awarded their kingship. King Billy's victory over the rejected Catholic King James at the Boyne in July 1690 was a victory of the Orange over the Green, because Catholic Irish fought alongside James's French in the battle — commemorated on July 12. (The Pope of the day supported King Billy in this adventure.)

Eleven months earlier King Billy's forces had lifted the long siege at Derry. After a handful of bold Apprentice Boys had shut the city gates against King James's Catholic troops, the mostly Protestant inhabitants of the city were starved nearly to death under a blockade by James's troops. This sense of seige persists among Protestants — the feeling of being surrounded, in their enclave in northeast Ireland, by alien and naturally inferior Irish Catholics.

The Catholic perception of the Orange Order was that its historical perspective and its whole mentality — including its fear of Catholics — was rooted in a bigotry carefully fostered by Protestant landlords in order to enlist the aid of poor Protestants in repressing the huge population of Catholic Irish. As for King William, Catholics didn't think much of him. But they didn't think that much about him either.

(Left) Ian Paisley at Apprentice Boys' Parade in Derry on 12 August 1981.

WOLFE TONE AND 1798. The Catholics' collective memory of Wolfe Tone was of a Protestant Irish rebel whose interest was in a united Ireland independent of Britain where all religions would live at peace with one another. Tone had written:

> To subvert the tyranny of our execrable Government, to break the connection with England, the never-failing source of all our political evils, and to assert the independence of my country — these were my objects.
> To unite the whole people of Ireland, to abolish the memory of all past dissensions, and to substitute the common name of Irishman in place of the denominations of Protestant, Catholic, and dissenter — these were my means . . .

Wolfe Tone was so persuasive an exponent of the Irish cause that in 1797 the French Directory sent several fleets and its finest general, Hoche, in support of Tone's revolutionary effort. But in 1797 and again in 1798 stormy seas undid Tone and the French invaders.

Ulster Protestants saw Wolfe Tone and Company as an example of what a handful of liberal Protestants could do to break down group discipline. Tone was anti-British; Ulster Protestants were British. Yet despite this loyalty, history showed many instances of Britain's cavalier attitude toward Ulstermen. As William Watson once put it, England had always "Jeered at her loyalty, trod on her pride,/Spurned her, repulsed her,/Great-hearted Ulster;/Flung her aside."

Protestants felt that Britain had only to look at the statements of a renegade like Wolfe Tone to realize how truly loyal the Protestants of Northern Ireland had been, and how deeply deserving they were of protection against Catholics and other nationalists who would try to force Protestants into some kind of independent Ireland.

HOME RULE. *The Protestant memory* of the nationalist Home Rule agitation was the memory of a series of major assaults on the right of Protestants to be and remain British. Charles Stewart Parnell, another Protestant turncoat, had the Catholics and his other allies diabolically well organized. The election in 1885 returned eighty-five Home Rulers out of a total of one hundred three Irish members of Parliament.

As evidence of Parnell's antipathy to Britain itself Ulster Protestants could cite his own reported words: "None of us . . . will be satisfied until we have destroyed the last link which keeps Ireland bound to England."

Protestant Orangemen of that era found allies, especially among English Conservatives and members of the House of Lords. Randolph Churchill, Winston's father, was an important English Conservative ally: "Ulster will fight," he said, "and Ulster will be right." Indeed, the Unionists of Ulster had already begun to arm themselves.

After the Home Rule bill was finally passed in 1912, Ulster Protestants imported large quantities of arms into Northern Ireland. They held monster rallies. Inspired by their Dublin-born champion, Edward Carson, they threatened Britain with

(Above) Members of the RUC pictured in May 1969 in riot gear. They wore visored helmets and carried body shields, batons and revolvers.

rebellion if Home Rule were ever applied in Ireland. "With the help of God," Carson said, "you and I joined together . . . will yet defeat the most nefarious conspiracy that has ever been hatched against a free people . . ."

The Catholic memory of Parnell was of a great Protestant Irishman who, if his legislation had not been undermined by the forces of Protestant wealth and privilege in Britain, could have probably brought Ireland its own parliament and eventual nationhood, and thus saved the nation from the bloodshed of the Easter Rising, the War of Independence and the Civil War, and prevented the tyranny of Protestant unionists over nationalist Catholics during the fifty years of Protestant sectarian rule in Northern Ireland.

For Catholics, what happened with the defeat of the Home Rule bills and the arming of the Ulster Volunteers by Carson — and the red-nosed whiskey distiller James Craig — was the postponement of the magnanimous Ireland Parnell believed in: "The class of Protestants will form a most valuable element in the Irish legislature of the future, constituting, as they will, a strong minority, and exercising a moderate influence in making laws . . . We want all creeds and classes in Ireland."

THE EASTER RISING AND THE WAR OF INDEPEN-
DENCE. *The Catholic perception* was roughly this: With the
Home Rule legislation on the books — to be shelved only
until the end of the First World War — one hundred sixty
thousand Irishmen responded to the nationalist leader John
Redmond's call to join the British forces and go fight "for
the freedom of small nations." Only a few thousand nationalist Irish Volunteers refused to wear British uniforms; they
stayed home and drilled and waited for a time when they
might fight to throw off the British yoke.

The Rising in 1916 — following Padraig Pearse's Easter
Monday proclamation of an Irish Republic at the General
Post Office in Dublin — was a short-lived affair. At the time
most Catholic Irish, because of the war in progress in Europe,
regarded the Rising and its perpetrators with scorn and
disgust.

But then the British killings began — the executions of the
leaders of the Easter Rising: Irish "traitors," the British called
them. Day after day, beginning on May 3, 1916, came news
or rumours of yet further summary executions of the leaders
of the Rising. On May 10, the British shot the last two. Under
the slow impact of these vindictive executions, Irish public
opinion turned dramatically from acceptance of the British
government in Ireland to revulsion against it. As one ballad
would put it:

> God's curse on you, England,
> You cruel-hearted monster,
> Your deeds they would shame
> All the devils in hell . . .

So the next year, when thirty-five hundred Irish men and
women who had played supporting roles in the Rising were
released from prisons in England and Wales, they returned to
a tumultous welcome in Dublin.

Among the freed prisoners was Michael Collins, now a
leader of a revolutionary secret society, the Irish Republican
Brotherhood. In 1918 he began shaping the Irish Republican
Army in what was to prove the most highly organized military
campaign in Irish history. By 1920 the IRA's flying columns
— hit-and-run cadres of locals in the Irish countryside — were
counter-terrorizing the tens of thousands of British police,
military and imported paramilitary terrorists — the brutal
"Black and Tans" (Winston Churchill's brain-children) and
the Auxiliaries. There were British reprisals and, particularly
from the paramilitary "Tans," further horrors and atrocities:
They burned and pillaged dozens of Irish towns and set fire
to half the city of Cork.

Meanwhile in Dublin key British spies and informers were
ruthlessly dispatched in sudden ambushes by Collins' assassination squad.

(Right) march on Falls Road, Belfast,
in April 1978, on the anniversary of the 1916 Easter
Rising.

Michael Collins organized, and the Irish local commanders fought, the first of the great guerrilla wars waged against Britain by her colonies. Just when the Irish revolution had nearly spent itself, the British decided — chiefly because of stories in English newspapers of British atrocities — to sue for peace. In July 1921 a truce was agreed, and by December a twenty-six county Irish Free State had been agreed.

But the six counties of Ulster were given over to the control of the Protestant unionists. Temporarily, it was thought. For Lloyd George had led Collins and the other treaty negotiators to believe that a Boundary Commission would transfer the large Catholic-majority portions of the six counties, including perhaps the whole of the Catholic-majority counties Fermanagh and Tyrone, to the Irish Free State. What was left of the six counties would be politically unviable, and would eventually be willing to join in an all-Ireland state.

The Protestant perception of the history of the period formed itself along very different lines. Counting the German weapons smuggled in at Larne and Bangor in April 1914, the Protestants of Ulster had a stock of forty thousand guns to oppose any concessions Britain might make to the South on the Home Rule issue. The war intervened, and some thirty-five thousand members of the hundred-thousand man Ulster Volunteer Force signed on with the British Army. These men, outfitted and equipped from UVF funds, covered themselves with glory fighting under the Union Jack in Europe. In the bloody Battle of the Somme, five and a half thousand men of the 36th (Ulster) Division were slaughtered or wounded during the first two days. The hard-fighting "Shankill Boys" battalion from West Belfast lost all but seventy of their original seven hundred men.

While Ulster Protestants were loyally fighting in Belgium and France, the disloyal Catholic Irish mounted their Easter Rising and their War of Independence; Ulster Protestants thought it was to Britain's everlasting shame that she caved in in 1921 to these men, traitors to their country, and allowed a Catholic-dominated Free State to be set up. Yet the Protestants of Ulster now reaped a political harvest from the blood sacrifice they had made during the war. They got their separate Northern parliament. It was Home Rule, but their own home rule, and they decided to make the best of it. They were helped by the fact that while they were getting their parliament underway, the Catholic Irish in the South were busy slaughtering one another in the brief but vicious 1922-23 Civil War.

(Left) Loyalist prisoners on roof of Crumlin Road jail demonstrating for better prison conditions in December 1981.

(Left) Bobby Jackson, well-known Derry personality, pictured in front of a street mural commemorating the lifting of the siege at Derry and victory in the Battle of the Boyne.

PARTITION AND THE NORTHERN IRELAND STATE. *The Protestant perception* of the Northern Ireland State set up in June 1921 was of nearly fifty years of peaceful and unionist majority government. In 1921 and 1922 there were bloody sectarian riots due to Catholic rebelliousness. More than five hundred and sixty people were dead by 1922. So it was necessary for the Northern Ireland government to raise and equip a large armed force of loyal Protestants: a regular police force, the Royal Ulster Constabulary (RUC) and a Special Constabulary of A, B and C ranks: The A-specials were later merged into the RUC and the C-specials disbanded, leaving only the B-specials.

Special powers had to be enacted to suppress the Catholic rebels; and changes had to be made in voting procedures, because Catholics in the North began using their votes to mark off enclaves loyal not to the new Northern Ireland government but to the Free State. So the legally constituted authority in Belfast, which of course was unionist Protestant, rearranged matters so that people loyal to the new government would be in control in all the important voting districts.

There remained the problem of the Boundary Commission.

Clearly the Commission had been arranged by the sly British with the intention of giving the Free State the extensive Catholic-majority portions of the six-county area, emasculating the Ulster State to the point where it would be unworkable, and bringing hundreds of thousands of loyal Protestant Ulstermen under Dublin's control. "What we have now, we hold," the Prime Minister James Craig said, and refused to cooperate. The Commission reported anyway, in 1925. But in the face of determined opposition from Northern Irish Protestants the border was left demarcated as in 1920.

Throughout fifty years, there was a democratically elected local Northern Ireland government. It built an impressive Parliament building at Stormont just outside Belfast. And, despite intermittent trouble from Catholics and their IRA, it had given the best leadership it could to the people of Northern Ireland, the vast majority of whom were Protestant unionists.

The Catholic view of partition and the Northern Ireland state was that both were based on a cruelly unjust gerrymander that put large majority Catholic areas under Protestant control. The 1921 and 1922 and later riots victimized Catholics, who were killed in such disproportionate numbers that what the riots amounted to was a racist Protestant suppression of Catholics in northeast Ireland.

For Catholics the Ulster State was not a matter of government by a democratically elected majority but of tyranny by a local majority under the domination of a Protestant elite. Catholics were treated as intruders in their own country; there was outrageous discrimination in matters like voting, housing and employment, with fully half the Catholic men in many areas in enforced unemployment. There was no freedom of speech or assembly for Catholics.

The North was a government of Protestant men of property and privilege who invoked the rhetoric and slogans of religious bigotry to get the Protestant working class to let them run Stormont to suit themselves. This Protestant power elite who ran the authoritarian statelet ground down poor Protestants as well as Catholics, using sectarianism and Orangeism to blind poor working class Protestants to their own miserable situation . . .

So ran the Catholic view.

(Right) Unionist Protestant leaders in 1966: Captain William Long, Brian Faulkner, William Craig.

So throughout the years Northern Ireland Catholics saw the Irish nation as incomplete, while Protestants saw themselves as threatened by "the nefarious conspiracy" that sought a united Ireland independent of Britain.

A condition of mutual resentment, fed perhaps as much by Protestant guilt as by Catholic grievance — a resentment triggered by the ritual and spontaneous recollection of vividly symbolic historical events — had to yield at some point to a physical struggle between the antagonists. There had been injustice. Something had to be done.

George Bernard Shaw had said, "Nothing is ever done in this world unless men are prepared to kill one another if it is not done."

Even from the Protestant point of view, it was an unnatural situation. It had to be resolved.

On October 5, 1968, came the confrontation that would prove to be the catalyst for the long-postponed conflict.

(Left) Loyalist wall in Sandy Row, Belfast, pictured in 1978.

(Right) Harry West marching in the Apprentice Boys' Parade in Derry on 12 August 1976.

The grievances of the Catholic minority were nearly all imaginary.

Harry West

(Left) RUC water cannon moving against Catholic youths in William Street near entry to the Bogside on 12 July 1969. Rossville Street is in right background.

3
The Two Antagonists

IN 1956-62 what was left of the physical force section of the Irish Republican Army had mounted a border campaign from the Republic of Ireland: This had been an attack on the Northern Ireland state. It was violence and was violently put down — by the predominantly Protestant RUC and the B-Specials. It was more easily put down because by the late 1950s the physical force advocates in the IRA had very little support left among the nationalist Catholic community for their violent approach to a solution, partly because earlier IRA activity had been so ineffectual while bringing the RUC and the hated "Specials" (the B-Specials of the police auxiliary) heavily down on Catholics generally.

So by 1962 the violent IRA was dead.

But Catholics, and some liberal- and labour-minded Protestants, saw a variety of social evils persisting in Northern Ireland: the blatant discrimination by Protestant-dominated industry and government in the allocation of housing and jobs; the still gerrymandered electoral districts; the rigging of voting qualifications to favour Protestants and exclude most Catholics; the denial of free speech and assembly. Catholics, who because of liberal legislation in Britain now had easy access to higher education, were emerging in numbers from the universities.

(Right) Soon the RUC in Derry would be out on the streets in riot gear, as in this photo taken six months later, in April 1969.

It was the era of Civil Rights. Looking at Northern Irish society they saw many similarities to the treatment given them by the dominant Protestants and the treatment given blacks by the dominant whites in the American South. It was, as Northern Irish Catholics and their Protestant supporters saw it, a matter of Catholics being denied equal opportunity, of being in fact, denied basic human rights. So in the late 1960s they founded a Northern Ireland Civil Rights Association. NICRA was non-republican and, although determined on a course of provocative civil disobedience, was nonetheless decidedly non-violent.

So the leaders of NICRA were modeling their protest not on the age-old Irish physical force tradition but on the very recent American civil rights movement. The American movement was not only non-violent and reformist; it took the shape of an *appeal* to the American government.

Accordingly, in the late 1960s, Northern Ireland civil rights leaders were calling not for the abolition of the existing Stormont government, but for its and Britain's *help* in remedying a variety of social and political evils.

On October 5, 1968, some two thousand people organized by NICRA gathered in Derry* for a major protest march in pursuit of their equal opportunity goals. The march had been banned by William Craig, the hardline Northern Ireland Minister for Home Affairs, on grounds the NICRA leaders considered specious.

Craig had ordered up large reinforcements of the RUC, whose orders were that they were not to allow the demonstrators to cross Craigavon bridge and march into the walled city. But the demonstrators, who felt the march had been unfairly banned, were willing to provoke retaliation if neces-

---

*"Londonderry" in official British usage, a usage favoured by most Protestants, though some favour the ancient name Derry, which has Protestant associations too (e.g., "the Apprentice Boys of Derry"). It was the name that the town had before the arrival in town and county (formerly the county of Coleraine, now Londonderry or Derry) of the often predatory London merchants, importers of evils like "brass money and wooden shoes." Moreover, Northern Ireland people are nothing if not succinct: so some Protestants, including many who live in Derry City, use Derry for brevity.

sary to show how their civil rights were being violated by the refusal to let them march within the symbolic walls.

They were fifty yards from the bridge when they found their way blocked by a line of police, supported by two mobile water cannons. Some marchers turned to withdraw, but found to their astonishment that other lines of police were blocking their retreat. Some marchers threw placards at the police. Some stones were thrown.

Then the RUC charged, and began attacking the demonstrators, brutally clubbing some of them with long batons. The RUC county inspector was seen on television — in Britain, in Ireland, in America and in living-rooms all over the world — lashing out violently at demonstrators with his blackthorn stick. Bernadette Devlin described the scene as she saw it:

> I had been watching the police and I'd seen them filter down on both sides of the march, so that now they encircled us. When we turned to go back down the street and re-form, we found we were trapped. There were policemen to the right and to the left, to the fore and the aft, and they just moved in on all four sides, with truncheons and heels and boots, and beat everybody off the street. Then the watercannons came out and hosed the streets.
>
> Quite deliberately they hosed in upstairs windows and shop-fronts, and they went right across Craigavon bridge, hosing all the onlookers. The police just went mad . . .
>
> While everyone was running madly round me, I was standing still — not because I hadn't panicked, but because panic had a different effect on me. I was standing .almost paralysed watching the expressions on the faces of the police. Arms and legs were flying everywhere, but what horrified me was the evil delight the police were showing as they beat people down, then beat them again to prevent them from getting up, then trailed them up and threw them on for somebody else to give them a thrashing. It was as though they had been waiting to do it for fifty years . . .

Protestants could and did argue that the march was illegal. Therefore Protestants who did not approve of the brutality could still stand behind the police, saying that the demonstrators, by conducting an illegal march and by their provocative actions, had brought the violence on themselves.

But what most Catholics — faced with this hostile reaction — tended to do, even those who disapproved of such demonstrations, was to rally behind the demonstrators. Derry Catholics formed an action committee. A students' civil rights group, People's Democracy, took shape at Queen's University in Belfast. Paisley began to organize a militant opposition.

For the new year 1969, the leftist People's Democracy group planned a long march from Belfast to Derry modeled on Martin Luther King's. The Civil Rights Association opposed the plan, but the leaders of People's Democracy felt that a march across Northern Ireland would test the Government's will: The marchers would have to be protected by the RUC from Protestant militants.

The marchers, eighty at first but a growing band, were mildly harassed by Paisleyite Protestant vigilantes and by police rerouting along the way. Still they continued. Then, on the morning of their last day, the marchers, now some five hundred in number, were only four miles from Derry City when they were escorted by the RUC onto Burntollet Bridge. A Protestant mob of two hundred — a hundred of whom were B-Specials in civilian clothes — waited on a hillside above. They charged down and ambushed the marchers, stoning and clubbing them into the fields and driving them into the river Faughan below. Some police protected the head of the march. Most police watched complacently, many of them sitting in their trucks, some of them openly delighted, as the marchers were attacked by the mob with stones and iron bars, bicycle chains and clubs with nails in them.

A great many of the marchers were injured. The survivors were attacked twice more before they reached Derry city. A thousand supporters went out to join them. There followed a rally of several thousand in Guildhall Square, where speakers

condemned the police of the RUC for their handling of the march.

Then, about two o'clock in the morning of January 5, a screaming and shouting mob of policemen, some of them drunk, came suddenly charging into the streets of the Catholic Bogside, smashing windows, kicking in doors, storming into homes, stoning and badly beating Catholics they got hold of.

In a subsequent inquiry the Stormont-appointed Cameron Commission found that the police were guilty that night of "assault and battery, malicious damage to property, and the use of provocative sectarian and political slogans."

Catholics who had originally opposed the People's Democracy march now formed a "citizens' army" in defence of the Bogside. John Hume, a moderate who was vice-president of the DCAC, told a thousand people at a rally that they should defend the area, and that no one should be allowed in or out.

The Bogsiders put up the barricades, and "Free Derry" was born as an area sealed off from police and later from other "security forces." In that time there arose the first new stirrings of the old Irish physical force republicanism. The boys of the Bogside waved a large tricolour from atop a flatblock, which confirmed many Protestants in their view that Catholics had used civil rights only as a cover, and that their real purpose all along had been to destroy the Northern Ireland state.

Most Protestants, and most members of their Protestant Unionist government, were angry. They felt that demonstrators were using both legal and illegal marches to *provoke* police and popular Protestant reaction. For years Terence O'Neill, the Stormont Prime Minister, had been showing goodwill towards Catholics. Hardliners, like the Rev. Ian Paisley whose supporters had led attacks on demonstrators at Burntollet and elsewhere, thought O'Neill was a milquetoast and said so.

> *The basic fear of the Protestants in Northern Ireland is that they will be outbred by the Roman Catholics. It is as simple as that. It is frightfully hard to explain to a Protestant that if you give Roman Catholics a good job and a good house they will live like Protestants, because they will see neighbours with cars and television sets. They will refuse to have eighteen children. But if the Roman Catholic is jobless and lives in a most ghastly hovel, he will rear eighteen children on national assistance. It is impossible to explain this to a militant Protestant because he is so keen to deny civil rights to his Roman Catholic neighbours. He cannot understand, in fact, that if you treat Roman Catholics with due consideration and kindness they will live like Protestants in spite of the authoritarian nature of their church.*
> *Terence O'Neill*

(Above)   RUC men in a baton charge at Waterloo Place in Derry, on 12 August 1969, at the beginning of the Battle of the Bogside.

(Left)   Terence O'Neill, Prime Minister of Northern Ireland, in broadcast following February 1969 general election.

For his involvement in illegal counter-demonstrations Paisley was jailed, angering his supporters. Unionist Party opinion was beginning to swing behind Paisley's and Craig's idea that Prime Minister O'Neill was too weak.

On April 17, 1969, the People's Democracy leader and civil rights activist Bernadette Devlin was elected to Westminster. On April 19 Paisleyites came to the city of Derry to flex their muscles, and bloody rioting again broke out.

Terence O'Neill, facing continuous challenges from Protestant and Unionist Party hardliners, finally quit. On May 1 he was replaced as leader of the Party by his cousin, Major James Chichester-Clark.

Against advice, Chichester-Clark decided to let the summertime Orange parades go forward as usual. Throughout Northern Ireland, riots followed the July 12 parades — in Belfast, in Derry, in Lurgan and in Dungiven. The B-Specials were mobilized. British Army units in Northern Ireland were put on alert. In Belfast, Catholic families living in mixed areas began moving out to Catholic neighbourhoods.

The divide between unionists and nationalists, between Protestants and Catholics, was becoming a chasm.

It was comparatively easy to understand the Catholics' growing sense of active grievance, now being fed by events themselves.

What of the Protestants? At first they were outraged at what they saw as an attack on their state by irresponsible republicans. They were angry that they, an honest, hard-working people, were being paraded across the television screens of the world as monsters of ruthless discrimination against Catholics. In addition to anger they were beginning to feel fear. Their way of life, their top-dog status in the little Northern Ireland state, seemed under threat. For many, it was the siege of Derry all over again. Protestants felt particularly unhappy because they knew that the accusations against them were well-founded: While they publicly denied that they were discriminatory towards Catholics, most privately admitted the fact. They of course felt justified in being discriminatory because they saw Catholics as dedicated to the overthrow of their state. Yet their consciences were nonetheless troubled and their half-hidden guilt made them angrier still.

In the run-up from April to mid-August 1969 there had been enough violence to keep the RUC and the B-Specials on edge. Yet the moderates among the Catholics and the calmer heads among the unionists and the police had kept the keg from blowing.

But Chichester-Clark convinced James Callaghan, the Home Secretary, that preventing the Apprentice Boys' Parade from going ahead in Derry would bring terrible repercussions from Protestants. This parade celebrated the defence of Derry, and symbolically of Northern Ireland, from the native Irish Catholic enemy. So Callaghan, despite predictions of violence from the Army and some police, told Chichester-Clark to go ahead.

On August 12 the parade in Derry began quietly. But in the afternoon, as the marchers were passing through Waterloo Place near the entrance to the Catholic Bogside area of the city, some teenage Catholic boys began throwing stones at them. The RUC chased the boys down into the Bogside — Protestants chasing Catholics as before; this time, though, the Catholic boys retaliated not with stones but with petrol bombs.

Remembering the police riots and brutality of October and January and April, the Derry Catholics — adults now joining in with the teenage boys — maintained a fierce defence of the Bogside. The police drew up more armoured cars and watercannon. They began to advance again on the Bogside barricades. The Bogsiders fought off the attack. Even some of the civil rights people encouraged the boys. Bernadette Devlin, the new member of Parliament, broke up paving stones for them to throw and led the fight on the principal battlefront. (The photographer Clive Limpkin took a picture of her doing this; he captioned it "Constituency work.")

Then some of the boys took up positions atop the highrise Rossville flats. This gave them suddenly a decisive military advantage over the attacking police. The fight raged on into the night. Down below the police responded, for the first time, with CS gas.

(Left) Ross McGlimpsie, RUC district inspector, surveys the scene as Protestants attack a civil rights marcher in the Diamond, in the center of the walled city of Derry, July 1969.

(Below) RUC man makes gesture towards Catholic youths at the time of the beginning of the battle of the Bogside in Derry, 13 August 1969.

The Protestant historian A.T.Q. Stewart described the physical picture from his point of view:

> After forty-eight hours a scene appeared in Derry which no one in Northern Ireland could remember seeing before, though something like it had happened more than once in the nineteenth century. Against a backdrop of blazing buildings, small groups of exhausted policemen huddled in doorways or lay in the streets, their faces streaked with blood and dirt, their tunics torn and even burned, like the weary survivors of some desperate and costly offensive . . .

The Bogsiders called — publicly on Irish television, and privately by telephone — for help: from the Irish of the Republic, from Belfast, from other towns in Northern Ireland. From across the border they got a few dozen freelance fighters. (Jack Lynch, the then Irish Taoiseach or Prime Minister, had the Irish Army set up a few hospital tents.)

From the other Northern Ireland towns they got enough disturbances to prevent the RUC from concentrating all its strength in Derry.

In Belfast, unlike Derry, Protestants far outnumbered Catholics, and many of the Catholic working-class communities were scattered among large surrounding districts of working-class Protestants or in mixed Catholic and Protestant neighbourhoods. It was in the mixed streets that much of the violence of the next days took place.

Beginning on the evening of August 13, a civil rights group walked up the Falls Road to present a petition complaining of police brutality in Derry at the Springfield Road RUC station. The petition was rejected by the RUC district inspector, who said it was not the "proper place" to present it. The procession began moving back down the road toward the Hastings Street RUC station to which they had been directed. Some youngsters began pelting the Springfield Road station with petrol bombs, but it was a relatively mild attack. No material damage was done. In response the RUC man in charge ordered several Shorland armoured cars into the streets.

If his objective was to frighten the Catholic petitioners, he certainly achieved it. They fled along the main roads and into the mixed side streets running northward toward the Protestant Shankill district. The Protestants in these streets, seeing Catholics running, decided that the Catholics were on the rampage, that the dreaded IRA was coming after them at last. Some of the crowd, in response to the armoured cars, went back to the Springfield Road police station and began attacking it, seriously this time. The RUC fired guns from the station. By now there were one or two people in the crowd with guns; they fired back at the RUC. The police apparently thought that the stone-throwers and the few petrol bombers were in the vanguard of a do-or-die attack on the RUC.

Next day the RUC armoured cars were reinforced by others. The police fitted some of them up with .30 calibre Browning machine guns. The Browning, a high velocity weapon which fired up to ten rounds a second, had a range of nearly two and a half *miles*.

61

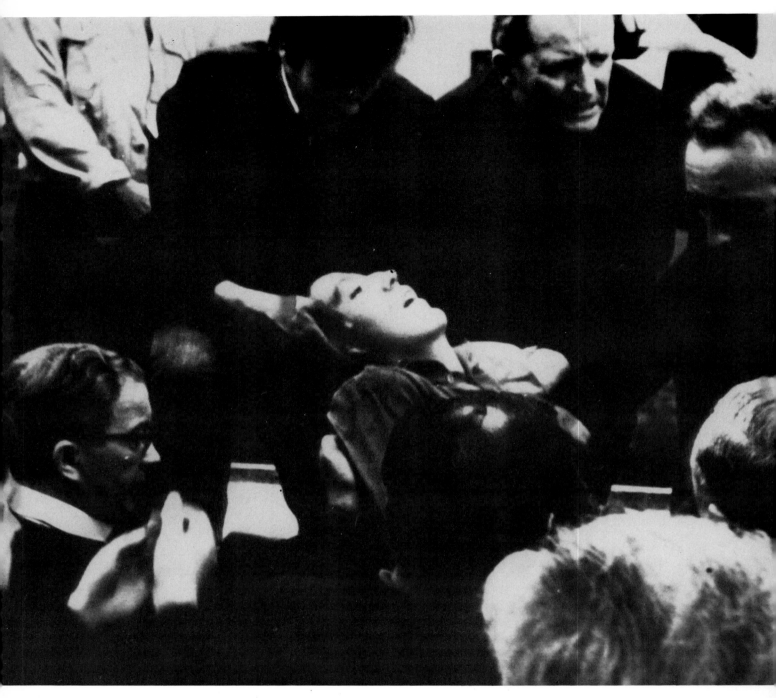

Meanwhile the B-Specials were in the streets, armed not with batons but with guns. Beginning the evening of the 14th, fierce fighting took place in the mixed streets running between the Falls and the Shankill Roads. In one confrontation a crowd of Catholic youths came up one of the mixed streets singing republican songs and carrying an Irish tricolour. Enraged, the Protestant crowd, B-Specials mingled among them, hurried down to terrorize the Catholics living at the Falls Road end of the street and began tossing petrol bombs into the doorways of Catholic houses.

(Above) Youth, caught in crossfire during rioting in Belfast on 15 August 1969, being taken to hospital.

It was after midnight when the RUC turned loose the machine-gun mounted armoured cars manned by ill-trained RUC officers. The RUC apparently thought that the rioting, especially in the Divis Street area at the bottom of the Falls Road, was part of an armed insurrection by Catholics. Catholics in the huge Divis Flats complex thought that they were being invaded by police. Barricades went up at Divis Flats and the RUC were showered with petrol bombs from the roof of one block of flats.

A Catholic school, Saint Comgall's, came under attack from Protestant petrol bombers. Then a burst of fire from an automatic rifle cut across Divis Street and hit a Protestant. Police nearby, hearing the burst of fire, opened fire themselves.

The men in the armoured cars decided that they were under attack from Divis Flats and began raking the flats with fire. Fifty rounds or more were poured into the Divis Flats from the Browning machine guns. At least thirteen flats were damaged. A British soldier, a Catholic home on leave, was out on his balcony; he was killed instantly. Four of the high velocity Browning bullets pierced two walls before finding a nine-year-old Catholic boy named Patrick Rooney asleep in his bedroom. The bullets took half the child's head away. Some of the Browning bullets missed Divis Flats and travelled two miles across the city, striking an RUC station; the police there were certain that the shooting signalled an IRA attack.

By the morning of August 15 some hundred fifty buildings and homes in the Divis Street and the Ardoyne District were devastated. Six people had been killed. Many Catholics packed their belongings and left the area, some of them taking the train to the Republic. Parts of Belfast were on fire. The rioting continued through the night of Friday, August 15, when Bombay Street was entirely burnt to the ground.

At this point Catholics had in the whole of Belfast some twenty-two usable guns. Virtually all the other guns (some hundred thousand of them) were in the hands of Protestants, especially members of the RUC and the B-Specials. Catholic defence was largely in the hands of teenagers with stones and petrol bombs. Catholics, however, had their anger, which grew and swelled over those five days from August 12 to August 16 to the point that most Catholic moderates in the cities joined the relative handful of militants in a single call to action.

"Get out the guns! Call in the fighters: Call in the IRA."

But there was no fighting IRA. There hadn't been for seven years.

Protestants had their own grounds for anger. Their peaceful march in Derry had been attacked by hooligans. Their police were fighting a pitched battle with the forces of anarchy and rebellion. An IRA rising had taken place in Belfast, Protestants told one another; the IRA was on the loose. And the Irish Army from the Republic was going to move in.

The Irish Army was not sent in. But the stage had been set for the advent of a new and much more heavily armed participant.

4

Help From Across the Water?

THE SITUATION had very sharply deteriorated between the time of the civil rights march on 5 October 1968 and mid-August 1969.

Political murders were taking place in Northern Ireland.

There was, of course, the fact of an economy starved of normal opportunity. Money, and the lack of it, and the lack of jobs and of what money could buy, was certainly one of the roots of this evil. The poverty. And this poverty was not only a Catholic problem. Poor Protestants, with miserable jobs, and miserable houses (the "mean abode in the Shankill Road") were little better off than poor Catholics.

To compensate the Protestant poor the landowners and businessmen who controlled the Northern Ireland state had given them a way of thinking that underlined their Protestantism, their Orangeism, their duty to vote Unionist to protect what little privilege they had from the disloyal Catholics and keep these Catholics "in their place," meaning keep the underdogs under.

But what was obvious to the commentators was that outside help was needed. And just as obvious to most of the commentators was the idea that the British were the people to sort this out. Many in Ireland, North and

South, believed this. And no wonder. Taking the two large islands as a whole, the British (fifty-five million) outnumber the Irish (nearly five million north and south) by a ratio of about eleven to one. So when the commentators were not themselves British, the dominant media noise was.

It was therefore judged that it was for the British to deal with this "tribal" conflict in Northern Ireland. Many even among the Catholic Irish, with their conservatism and their deeply ingrained sense of propriety, believed this themselves. Why not? they asked. Weren't the British the sovereign government up there in the North? That's what the media kept saying.

And so the British came, to sort out the problem among the warring tribes.

The British, however, came burdened with their own luggage of symbolic imagery. There was the notion — sustained perhaps as much by the requirements of propaganda as by any real conviction — that their honour required their involvement as disinterested intermediary in Northern Ireland.

There were other factors, too, in the mindset the British brought to their role in the conflict.

The British felt they had significant proprietary, economic, military, emotional and strategic interests in Northern Ireland.

There was of course among many Britons the matter of hanging onto this remnant (or tatter) of what was as recently as 1935 a world-girdling empire: the emotional but nonetheless real matter of imperial pride. The United Kingdom was precisely "The United Kingdom of Great Britain and Northern Ireland."

There was the economic consideration: Ireland was an important source of funds for certain British landowners and industrialists whose tenure and incomes might not be as secure if, for example, Northern Ireland were to become part of an all-Ireland Republic. There was the economic supply factor. Northern Ireland provided agricultural and industrial goods for what the British called "the mainland" — i.e., the larger island of Britain itself.

(Left)   British soldiers of 1st Gloustershire Regiment on patrol near Belfast "peace line," 1969.

67

Besides all that, Ireland, south as well as north, had been a dependable source of soldiers for the British Army and of sailors for the Royal Navy. Indeed, British awareness of Ireland had always had a military note about it. It was seen either as providing dependable recruits for the imperial colonial machine (it is in this connection that the British seem to have coined the term, "the fighting Irish") or as presenting a military problem. The Irish throughout the centuries were, in the British view, always unduly bellicose, always having to be subdued and reconquered.

The British Army Brigadier Frank Kitson found in the current conflict a reminder of the kind of law and order problem the British had been facing in Ireland for centuries: "In the historical context it may be of interest to recall that when the regular army was first raised in the seventeenth century 'Suppression of the Irish' was coupled with 'Defence of the Protestant Religion' as one of the two main reasons for its existence."

Such considerations — what might be called the Cromwellian view — had always figured in the British calculus about Ireland.

(Right)   British soldier with grenade gun in Derry, 1969.

(Below)   Harold Wilson pictured at Aldergrove Air Force base near Belfast on 15 November 1971. Wilson had been British Prime Minister in 1968-70 at the beginning of the conflict, and again later in 1974-76.

And Kitson's remarks also carry another characteristic note — of being affronted by the propensity of the Irish for unsuitable violence (*unsupervised* "fighting Irish"!)

Partly as a corollary England, and latterly Britain, had always had a sense of Ireland as a burden. "It is quite plain," the Earl of Roden wrote in 1835, "that ordinary laws calculated for civilized communities are not applicable to a country so circumstanced." It was always, tiresomely, "England's Irish Problem."

The vague fear that an enemy of Britain might use a hostile or even a neutral Ireland as a convenient base from which to menace or attack Britain had often played an important part in the British view of Ireland and Northern Ireland.

Intermittently this fear took sharper definition — as for example in a confidential document circulated by the Commonwealth Relations Office in 1951:

> Historically, Ireland, which has never been able to protect herself against invasion, has been, as she is today, a potential base for attack on the United Kingdom. It is the more important that a part of the island, and that one strategically well placed, should, and of its own free will, wish to remain part of the United Kingdom and of the United Kingdom defence scheme.
>
> Experience in the last war showed that, because of Eire's neutrality and her consequent denial of facilities for anti-submarine patrolling and the protection of shipping using the south-western approaches, it was of vital strategic importance to the Allies to hold the Six Counties and so command of the north-western approaches, the use of which was essential for the feeding and supplying of the United Kingdom and for the reinforcing of Allied troops based on the United Kingdom.
>
> A United Ireland whose willing and unqualified co-operation could not with certainty be relied on, which was neutral, or which was sharply divided internally over neutrality, would be a major problem in the defence of the United Kingdom and in the defence and support of Western Europe.

The British felt they were beyond the threadbare historical considerations that animated the Protestant and Catholic antagonists. Their view of Ireland was often aggressively a-historical.

Despite their detached view of history, the British were of course aware of certain historical landmarks. They were aware that the new conflict had arisen from the ancient quarrel between Protestant and Catholic Irishmen. They had to be aware that they hadn't resolved this quarrel, that they had in fact set the arena for it.

(Above) Red-capped British military policemen being welcomed by Catholic children in the Creggan area of Derry on 14 October 1969.

The English have every reason to feel proud of their country's recent record in Northern Ireland, since it sets the whole world a uniquely impressive example of altruistic service in the cause of peace. Nothing done by any other country in modern times so richly deserves the Nobel prize . . .

The British do not have their heart in Northern Ireland. The spur is duty, not love or affection or even interest. What other country would be prepared, year after year, to shoulder a burden the weight of which cannot be lightened by any propaganda sleight of hand about its noble contents? . . .

This, I think, is where the IRA makes its great mistake: in underestimating the maturity of the British people, their unique capacity to carry on without the kind of sentimental uplift which less adult breeds find so essential for sustained resolve and sacrifice. The IRA takes it for granted that sooner or later the people in this country will lose heart in the cause. But the truth is that they have never had any heart in the cause to lose. But they have something else, which is deeper, and much more difficult to lose: an inescapable sense of obligation. Hearts are easily broken and melted. If the British were in Northern Ireland out of affection or affinity, then the case for withdrawal would have long since become overwhelming. But they are not there out of affection and affinity. They are there in honour bound, because there is no escape which would not lead to a bloodbath.

Peregrine Worsthorne
Sunday Telegraph/*3 May 1981*

The moment the very name of Ireland is mentioned, the English seem to bid adieu to common feeling, common prudence and common sense and to act with the barbarity of tyrants and the fatuity of idiots.

Sydney Smith
1807

> *When the Ulster settlements were made, there was an implied compact that they who crossed the Irish Sea on what was believed to be a great colonizing and civilizing mission should not in themselves, nor in their descendants, be abandoned to those who regarded them as intruders, and as enemies.*
> *David W. Miller*

There was a certain, even outspoken conviction that they had not always *managed* Ireland properly. Many acknowledged that the high point of their mismanagement had come in the Great Famine during the middle of the nineteenth century that halved the population of Ireland through starvation and emigration. Some Britons realized that had they handled the Home Rule business better there would never have been an Easter Rising or an Irish War of Independence (1918-21). Yet the British as a whole had always felt under a kind of contractual obligation to support the unionist Protestant faction. Because of this contract or compact, backed by Protestant Irish threats of rebellion, a British government had set up the six-county state in the first place.

Yet the British had to regard the Protestants, staunch supporters of union and Empire — who had proved it by giving their lives at the Somme and elsewhere — as their natural adherents.

They could not be overenthusiastic about a Northern Irish Catholic people who had made a show of them before the whole world: people whose cousins in the South had been the first of many subject peoples to rebel against the British Empire. Certainly the British had to have their preferences in this matter.

True, this attitude was beginning to be re-examined. The South had proved over the years since World War II to be a dependable sort of provincial market for British goods, and a nice, safe haven for British capital and industry, as well as a pleasant place to visit during summer holidays. In fact, as far as British investment in the South was concerned, it was overtaking British investment in Northern Ireland.

In any event, the British found themselves obliged to give Northern Ireland attention and energy that they would have preferred to put to some less controversial and more profitable purpose. Nor were they entirely sure, given their past problems with Ireland, that they could sort out the natives over there, even now. Yet they felt honour bound to try. It was their patriotic duty. Jim Prior was to say, in September 1981, on accepting Margaret Thatcher's Greek gift of the Northern Ireland secretaryship, that the conflict presented "a very difficult national and international problem to everyone who lived in the United Kingdom and beyond." "If you are asked to do a job," he said, "you put your country first": patriotism and national *honour*.

(Right) James Callaghan, British Home Secretary at the start of the conflict, visits the Fountain Street area of Derry in October 1969. Callaghan is accompanied by Sir Arthur Young, then RUC chief constable, and Albert Anderson, a Stormont MP.

The British were aware of how the Northern Ireland conflict had developed: the problem of the Catholics as a deprived minority within a majority Protestant state: the problem of the Protestants as a threatened minority surrounded by an overwhelmingly Catholic majority on the island of Ireland: the double minority problem. They approached the Irish with a certain wariness: "You will never get to the bottom of this most perplexing and damnable country," H.H. Asquith had written to his wife in 1916.

So it was with trepidation, as well as with a certain jaunty confidence, that the British government turned once again to that age-old Irish Question in its newest form.

Army observation posts at Her Majesty's Prison the
Maze at Long Kesh near Belfast in 1981.

11
A Regime of Violence

That corpse you planted
  last year in your garden,
Has it begun to sprout?
Will it bloom this year?
              T.S. Eliot

(Left) British soldier crouching beneath Free Derry wall. They are under attack from Catholic youths following British Army killings of two unarmed Catholic men, Seamus Cusack and Desmond Beattie, in July 1977.

5
The Third Antagonist

BEGINNING IN mid-August 1969 the British Government came by stages to enmesh itself and the British Army in the conflict.

Britain controlled weaponry and engines of destruction far more lethal than those possessed by the combination of other participants.

In all subsequent events up to the end of January 1972, three turning points could be considered crucial: the Falls Road curfew, internment and Bloody Sunday.

The British Army was careful at first not to provoke either Protestants or Catholics. There were skirmishes between the Army and members of both Northern Irish communities and, beginning in late autumn 1969, more serious confrontations. But the Army was kept under more or less tight rein. Then, in June 1970, the British Labour Government was replaced by a Conservative Government. The man in charge from mid-1970 until early 1972 was Reginald Maudling, the Tory Government Home Secretary. Immediately he announced a "get tough" policy to deal with annoyances from Catholic youths and a few gunmen. (The Provisional IRA, formed in late 1969, was now mildly active, as were some members of the marxist Official IRA.)

As a direct result of the new policy the British Army was brought down like a hammer on the hapless Catholics of West Belfast.

For the Catholics and the British Army the crunch came at four-thirty on the evening of July 3. The Army had been tipped off that weapons would be found in a Catholic house at 24 Balkan Street, in a working class area off the Lower Falls Road. But the arms search, because of panicky Army management, escalated in a series of leaps into a major confrontation between the British Army and an entire section of

(Below) A local man is searched during the Falls Road curfew in Belfast in July 1970.

the population of Belfast. Troops went to the rescue of trapped troops, and the rescuers in turn had to be rescued.

Sir Ian Freeland, the British GOC in Northern Ireland, used his soldiers to cordon off the whole area. Once Freeland had cordoned it he ordered his men to *invade* the Lower Falls. They did.

An hour and a half after the invasion, Freeland declared a curfew for the Lower Falls, and ordered troops to conduct a house-to-house arms search of the entire area. Troops busied themselves through the weekend ripping out floorboards,

(Below) Reginald Maudling (right), then British Home Secretary, at RAF Air Base at Aldergrove in December 1971. With him at left is Keith McDowall, a press officer.

staircases, fireplaces, ceilings. In the end they reported finding two hundred eight guns, twenty-one thousand rounds of ammunition, two hundred fifty pounds of explosives and eight two-way radios. The cost of these limited discoveries was high. In the two and a half days that began with the Balkan Street episode, five civilians were killed. The army had managed to alienate, outrage and radicalize what had until then been a largely neutral Catholic populace.

Things could never be the same again between the Catholic people of Belfast and the British Army. The Falls Road debacle and its aftermath brought a flood of recruits to the Belfast IRA.

In 1971, the nascent Provos, who now *were* getting guns, began to attack police and troops and commercial targets. There were a number of killings. In March, three young off-duty Scottish soldiers were shot dead; Chichester-Clark resigned and a hardline Protestant businessman, Brian Faulkner, became Prime Minister of Northern Ireland. Faulkner firmly believed that internment was the way to destroy the IRA.

On July 8, 1971 in Derry, two unarmed Catholic men, Seamus Cusack and Desmond Beattie, were shot dead by British troops.

Army public relations put out word that the men were armed gunmen. The British press echoed this. The local people knew they were not. The government refused Catholic demands to set up a public inquiry into the circumstances of these killings, and the largely Catholic SDLP (Social Democratic and Labour Party) walked out of the Stormont Parliament in protest at this refusal.

On July 16, the SDLP announced they were going to set up their own "non-sectarian non-unionist assembly."

In Derry, as in Belfast, there was a new resurgence of support for the paramilitaries, provoked by the way British troops had been used and by the way British officialdom and a slavishly jingo British press covered up for them.

Eamonn McCann wrote:

> Speakers made a straightforward appeal to "Join the IRA." Afterwards, applicants for membership formed a queue. If the army was going to shoot us down unarmed, if they were going to lie about it afterwards, if the press was going to print the lies as fact, and if cabinet ministers in London were going to lie in their teeth in the Commons to cover up, there was only one answer . . .

Ian Paisley's newspaper, *The Protestant Telegraph*, mirroring hardline unionist reaction to the events of the period, insisted that "The vermin must be suppressed either by internment or effective action by our security forces."

(Above) Brian Faulkner, who had been Stormont Prime Minister during the time of internment. The civil rights militant John McGuffin described Faulkner as "a bitter, treacherous man, disliked and mistrusted by all"; according to the Belfast Catholic politician Paddy Devlin, Faulkner was a man who in the Sunningdale phase made a "celebrated debut as the most effective reformer in the North in the last fifty years."

As Stormont Minister of Home Affairs a decade earlier, Brian Faulkner had made internment work against the IRA of that era. In July, despite the opposition of most British Army leaders and of many of his own cabinet and party, Faulkner managed to sell the internment idea to the British Government. "We are at war with the IRA," Faulkner declared. By internment was meant the seizure without notice of terrorist "suspects" — virtually all of whom were Catholic — and their imprisonment without arrest warrant and without trial.

Just after four in the morning on August 9, British soldiers swooped down on houses all over Northern Ireland. That day they arrested three hundred forty-two men, most of them innocent of all connection with the IRA, many of them sole supporters of their households.

In the ghettoes of Derry, the people of the neighbourhoods poured out into the narrow streets to inhibit the Army sweep.

In Belfast the women banged dustbin lids on the pavement to alert neighbour households; older men and boys pushed huge rubbish tips down the road, overturned and set fire to large lorries and buses to block the soldiers' path.

From August until December, 1971, fifteen hundred seventy six men in all were arrested.

Within forty-eight hours after that first sweep, the Army (in pursuit of good public relations!) released one hundred sixteen of the prisoners.

But from some of these released men came shocking stories of what had happened to them in the prison cages. They had been beaten, had had guns with blank cartridges fired off behind their heads, had been forced to run the gauntlet of soldiers hitting them with cudgels, had been driven barefoot over broken glass. Some of the men were pushed blindfolded backwards out of helicopters they were told were high up in the air.

A further fourteen men, detained for longer periods, told of sensory deprivation and sensory overload techniques,

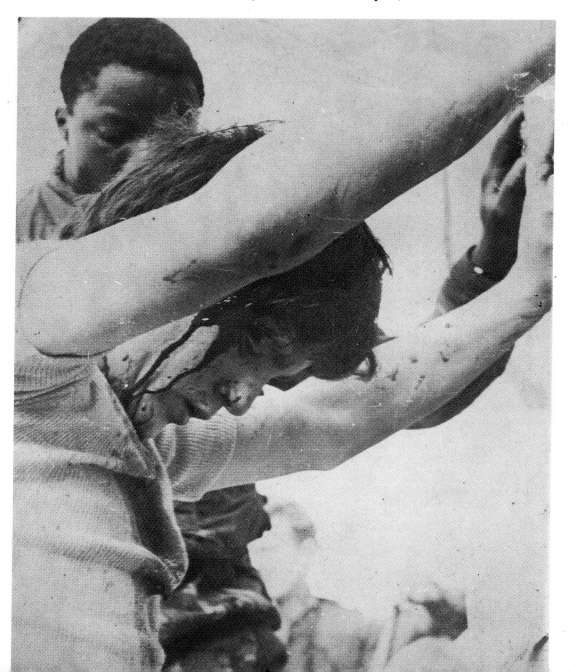

including white noise designed to convince a prisoner that he had gone mad. Spread-eagled against walls, they were kicked and beaten by their tormentors. They were deprived of food and sleep for long periods, during which they were interrogated mercilessly. There was more.

The following is one list of methods the British Army and the Royal Ulster Constabulary used:

> Placing a man in "search position," single finger of each hand to the wall, legs well apart and well back, on the toes, knees bent, for prolonged periods; heavy punching to the pit of the stomach of man in "search position."
>
> Kicking between the legs while in the "search position." so that he falls to the ground, banging his head on the wall, radiator or ground; beating with batons on the kidneys and on the privates of men in "search position."
>
> Kicking between the legs while in the "search position". This is very popular among the RUC officers and they often do it for periods of half an hour or an hour; putting a man in "search position" over a very powerful electric fire or radiator.
>
> Stretching a man over benches with two electric fires underneath and kicking him in the stomach; rabbit punching to the back of the neck while in "search position"; banging the head against the wall.
>
> Beating the head with a baton in crescendo fashion; slapping the ears and face with open hand; twisting the arms behind the back and twisting fingers; prodding the stomach with straight fingers.
>
> Chopping blows to the ribs from behind with simultaneous blows to the stomach; hand squeezing of the testicles; kicking of the knees and shins; tossing the prisoner from one officer to the other and punching him while in the air; deprivation of sleep.
>
> Psychological tortures:
> Russian roulette; firing blanks; beating men in darkness; blindfolding; assailants using stocking masks or wearing surgical dress; prisoners made to stare at white perforated wall in small cubicle; prisoners threatened; threats to their families; offering of bribes; use of false confessions.

That list comes from Denis Faul and Raymond Murray, who also listed methods that were only rarely used such as inserting instruments in the anal passage (a very common practice in later years with prison warders searching H-Blocks prisoners); the use of injections and amphetamine drugs; the use of electric cattle prods and other machines to give prisoners electric shocks, and the burning of prisoners' flesh with matches and candles. The list of methods furnished in the British Government's Compton Report, though presented with a view to defending the use of torture, was scarcely less chilling.

(Left) A Derry boy, Billy McIntyre, 16, after being arrested and beaten by soldiers at the time of internment in late 1971. There were no charges against the teenage McIntyre and he was released soon afterward

In response to reports about what was going on in the interrogation centres, the English novelist Graham Greene wrote:

> "Deep interrogation" — a bureaucratic phrase which takes the place of the simpler word "torture" and is worthy of Orwell's 1984 — is on a different level of immorality than hysterical sadism or the indiscriminate bomb of urban guerrillas. It is something organized with imagination and a knowledge of psychology, calculated and cold-blooded . . .

By the end of 1971 interrogatory torture and brutality had become established features of life in Northern Ireland.

Faulkner's enthusiasm explained internment. But what explained torture? There is no question but that Brigadier Frank Kitson had some interest, and was involved in all this from the very beginning. Kitson's theories of "low intensity" modern urban warfare — learned partly from British dealings with colonial upsets elsewhere in the world (in the Mediterranean, the Middle East and Africa), partly from the Korean war, partly from American tactics in Vietnam, and most importantly from studies of the KGB — were theories that he wanted to test in Northern Ireland.

One of Kitson's notions was that the Army should use political and psychological as well as directly military tools and techniques.

(Above) A young man is arrested by soldiers during an anti-internment civil rights march from Dungannon, Co. Tyrone, to Coalisland, on 29 January 1972.

(Right) Brigadier — now General — Frank Kitson, pictured in November 1971 when he was commanding officer of the 19th Airportable Brigade in Northern Ireland.

But saddling Kitson with entire responsibility is a mistake. The whole scheme of interrogatory torture *as experimentation* was carefully organized on orders from authorities of far higher rank than Kitson. A seminar was conducted at an English military school, with instruction in sensory deprivation techniques and on their application in Northern Ireland. The exercise was supervised by personnel from British Army intelligence; British Naval intelligence was also involved and, to a lesser extent, RAF intelligence. Some Tory politicians took an active interest.

British policy as a whole extended beyond the use of techniques of torture and brainwashing. Military specialists of the MRF (Military Reconnaissance Force, also called Military Reaction Force) and of the SAS were later sent around to murder suspects on sight, or to kill or mutilate local people in such a way that other locals would be blamed, and to create havoc in ethnic neighbourhoods in an attempt to force people to yield up the terrorists they shielded. Kitson's theory and British practice also provided for Army propaganda cadres which would spread lies and half-truths to discredit politicians and paramilitaries of both local communities.

The use in Northern Ireland of methods that would be completely unacceptable on the "mainland" of Britain has been attributed to various factors, all of which played a part: to political ignorance; to political incompetence; to a deliberate effort to "soften up" the nationalist Catholic community; to the Army's inexperience in dealing with the frustrations of civil disturbance in a "foreign" part of the United Kingdom; to a deliberate use of Northern Ireland as a laboratory for the testing and "improvement" of new techniques of interrogation.

In all this there was gross political insensitivity. The gathering of vast amounts of low-grade intelligence was embarked on with the aim of building an overall profile of the working-class Catholic population, and without concern for the fact that the methods themselves alienated that population.

There was no question about it: The British, by lending Faulkner the Army enforcers who carried out internment, and by themselves introducing torture, had written an exponent into the calculus of violence. Northern Ireland erupted into something very like civil war: It was Catholics now versus the "legitimate" authorities — unionist Protestant and British — and their various military wings: the Army, the now rearmed RUC, the UDR (Ulster Defence Regiment) and the RUC reserve.

Catholic politicians had walked out of Stormont and resigned their positions on other public bodies. Ordinary Catholics staged industrial strikes, rent and rates strikes. And now the Catholic bombers and gunmen were taking to the streets with a vengeance.

In the four months before internment, four civilians were killed in Northern Ireland, four soldiers and no policemen: a total of eight people. In the four months after internment seventy-three civilians were killed along with thirty soldiers and eleven policemen: a total of one hundred fourteen people.

The facts and figures of deaths and injuries, explosions and widespread destruction and disorder sparked off by these actions of the British Army (and the RUC) read like a horror story to James Callaghan, now no longer the minister in charge of British activities in Northern Ireland. "Was it necessary to wade through this river of blood?" Callaghan asked.

The spiralling violence, which had grown since August 1969, was now promoted in the autumn of 1971 to the dimensions of a dizzying vortex.

Internment, coupled with the introduction of torture, was proving disastrous for a British Government which was getting loud and suddenly worldwide criticism for the violence in Northern Ireland. Suddenly, too, its Army was the *principal* military antagonist. The British could no longer pose as mediator, sitting godlike above the battle.

The Army was increasingly seen as a partisan force, as being used chiefly against Catholics. Only a single incident was needed to register vividly how fiercely partisan the British Army could be. That incident occurred before the first month of the new year had passed — with the Army's intervention in a demonstration against internment at Derry.

The day was Sunday, January 30, 1972.

(Above)   Battered Magilligan Strand marcher being helped by a fellow demonstrator.

Internment was a calculated humiliation which unionist governments had, since the inception of the state, regularly visited upon our community. In the twenties, the thirties, the forties and the fifties, the RUC had come storming into our areas at night, dragged our people from their beds and taken them off to camps and prison ships, where they were often held for years, no charge, no trial, nothing. There was not a family in the area which had not had a relative or a neighbour interned. Now it was happening again . . .

Eamonn McCann

On Saturday, January 22, anti-internment demonstrators had marched to Magilligan camp, designed for some of the internees swept up by the British Army during the previous five months. The Magilligan marchers were met by the British Army's 1st Parachute battalion. As the crowd moved towards the camp the Paras fired rubber bullets, then clubbed and gassed the marchers, stopping them on the approaches to the camp. This embittered feelings between the Paras and local Catholics.

(Below) Paratroopers attacking civilians during anti-internment march at Magilligan Strand on 22 January 1972.

It was difficult to discover afterwards who ultimately approved the Paras' behaviour eight days later — on Sunday the 30th. Clearly the Unionist Government and Army leaders intended that the Paras use force against Derry Catholics gathered for another demonstration against internment.

That Sunday, the Provisional and Official wings of the IRA had both seen to it that no demonstrators were armed. But then, as the protest demonstration began to break up, the Catholic demonstrators were suddenly and unexpectedly assaulted by the Paras, who leapt from their tenders firing guns into the crowd. They kept firing them as they chased the Catholics into the Bogside.

After half an hour they had shot some two dozen people, killing thirteen men and boys (another man died later), all of them unarmed.

(Above) Youth in Derry being chased by a paratrooper armed with gun and baton on Bloody Sunday, 30 January 1972.

An English Chief Justice, one Lord Widgery, conducted an investigation in which he virtually white-washed the paratroops. The perfection of the British Establishment's propaganda instrument was perhaps never so clearly indicated as in the aftermath of the Bloody Sunday massacre. In London the BBC announced that gunmen and bombers had opened up on troops in Derry, forcing the troops to retaliate. Two days later the British Government information service issued a long "policy background" statement that asserted among other things:

Of the thirteen men killed in the shooting that began after the bulk of the three thousand marchers had been peacefully dispersed, four were on the security forces' wanted list. One man had four nail bombs in his pocket. All were between the ages of sixteen and forty.

The shooting started with two high-velocity shots aimed at the troops manning the barriers. No one was hit and fire was not returned. Four minutes later a further high-velocity shot was aimed at a battalion wire-cutting party. This shot also was not answered.

A few minutes later a member of the machine-gun platoon saw a man about to light a nail bomb. As the man prepared to throw, an order was made to shoot him. He fell and was dragged away.

Throughout the fighting that ensued, the Army fired only at identified targets — at attacking gunmen and bombers. At all times the soldiers obeyed their standing instructions to fire only in self-defence or in defence of others threatened.

The bulk of the marchers dispersed after reaching the barricades, on instructions from the march stewards. A hard core of hooligans remained behind and attacked three of the barriers. When the attacks reached an unacceptable level, the soldiers were ordered to pass through and arrest as many as possible. They were not, however, to conduct a running battle down the street.

As they went through the barriers the soldiers fired rubber bullets to clear the streets in front of them. They made forty-three arrests.

The troops then came under indiscriminate firing from apartments and a car park. The following is the army's account of the return fire:

(1) nail-bomber hit in the thigh; (2) petrol-bomber apparently killed in the car park; (3) bomber in the flats, apparently killed; (4) gunman with pistol behind barricade, shot and hit; (5) nail-bomber shot and hit; (6) another nail-bomber shot and hit; (7) rubber bullet fired at gunman handling pistol; (8) nail-bomber hit; (9) three nail-bombers, all hit; (10) two gunmen with pistols, one hit, one unhurt; (11) one sniper in a toilet window fired on and not hit; (12) gunman with pistol in 3rd floor flat shot and possibly hit; (13) gunman with rifle on ground floor of flats shot and hit; (14) gunman with rifle at barricade killed and body recovered . . .

Three months later Widgery, after concluding his "hearings" on what had happened, declared that the paratroops had not fired until fired upon and that some of the victims had almost certainly been armed.

The poet Thomas Kinsella describes being in Philadelphia

> on the first anniversary of Bloody Sunday; a local group picketed the BOAC office on Kennedy Boulevard, having failed to solve the problem of picketing the British Consulate on the fifteenth floor of a nearby office block. The event was mentioned briefly on the radio, with the explanation that on Bloody Sunday the previous year a gun battle had broken out in Londonderry between the IRA and the British army and that thirteen IRA gunmen had been killed.
>
> Explanatory matter of this kind is supplied on request by the British Information Service in the United States; where else would a harassed news editor turn, reporting on the same day the return of American troops from Vietnam? There is no Irish news agency . . .

It was in the ironic passages in his poem *Butcher's Dozen* that Kinsella had written perhaps the best extant commentary on the British fabrications — military, journalistic and juristic — about Bloody Sunday. The poet, returning to the scene of the massacre, interviews one of the dead victims:

> 'A bomber I. I traveled light
> —Four pounds of nails and gelignite
> About my person, hid so well
> They seemed to vanish where I fell.
> When the bullet stopped my breath
> A doctor sought the cause of death.
> He upped my shirt, undid my fly,
> Twice he moved my limbs awry,
> And noticed nothing. By and by
> A soldier, with his sharper eye,
> Beheld the four elusive rockets
> Stuffed in my coat and trouser pockets.
> Yes, they may be strict with us,
> Even in death so treacherous!'

But the television camera was there, and the people of Derry, and their priests. So Kinsella, through the mouth of another victim, lets the irony roll out into sarcasm:

> 'Yet England, even as you lie,
> You give the facts that you deny.
> Spread the lie with all your power
> — All that's left; it's turning sour.
> Friend and stranger, bride and brother
> Son and sister, father, mother,
> All not blinded by your smoke,
> Photographers who caught your stroke,
> The priests who blessed our bodies, spoke
> And wagged our blood in the world's face.
> The truth will out, to your disgrace . . .'

(Above) John Passmore Widgery, Lord Chief Justice of England, pictured in August 1972.

(Left)   Barney McGuigan before being murdered.

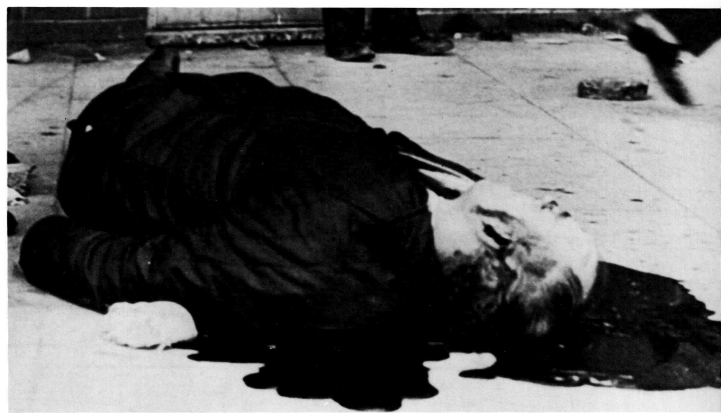

(Above)   Barney McGuigan, a victim of paratroop gunmen, lying dead in a pool of his own blood on Bloody Sunday, 30 January 1972.

Talking about his motives for writing the poem, subtitled "A Lesson for the Octave of Widgery," Kinsella underscores the appositeness of the judge's name:

Butcher's Dozen was not written in response to the shooting of the thirteen dead in Derry. There are too many dead, on all sides, and it is no use pitting them hideously against one another. The poem was written in response to the Report of the Widgery Tribunal. In Lord Widgery's cold putting aside of truth, the nth in a series of expedient falsehoods — with Injustice literally wigged out as Justice — it was evident to me that we were suddenly very close to the operations of the evil real causes . . .

The National Council for Civil Liberties of Britain — an affiliate of the International League for the Rights of Man — brought in a special investigatory team of its own. The man who wrote the civil liberties' indictment, titled *Justice Denied*, was the American criminal lawyer Sam Dash, who later became famous as a US congressional committee prosecutor in the Watergate case. Dash found, among other things that

> The thirteen known civilian dead were unarmed when they were killed on January 31, 1972, in Londonderry, and that they were shot either recklessly or deliberately by paratroopers of the First Battalion Parachute Regiment . . .

The Londonderry city coroner said at the end of his inquest into the deaths of the victims:

> It strikes me that the Army ran amok that day and they shot without thinking of what they were doing. They were shooting innocent people. These people may have been taking part in a parade that was banned — but I don't think that justifies the firing of live rounds indiscriminately. I say it without reservation — it was sheer unadulterated murder.

There was ample evidence, however, that the Paras had not run amok — that they were under orders to come out shooting. The massacre was so obviously a deliberate and premeditated attack that it stirred a fierce anger even in moderate Catholics: "For the Catholics of the Bogside," John Hume said, "it's a united Ireland now, or nothing." The Catholic paramilitaries vowed renewed and terrible violence.

(Above)   Londonderry City Coroner Hubert O'Neill at the Bloody Sunday inquest, 21 August 1973.

(Right)   Coffins in place for funeral mass at Creggan Chapel, Derry, for the men and boys killed by paratroopers on Bloody Sunday.

But the very fact that internment and the paratroop mass-acre on Bloody Sunday so stirred Catholics, and Catholic fury and promises of revenge, led to violent counter-repercussions across the ethnic divide. A Protestant woman — or so the signature on the letter read — expressed a widely-felt Protestant reaction in the February 1972 issue of the *Bulletin* of the newly-formed Ulster Defence Association (UDA):

(Above) **Monster rally organized by unionist leaders at Ormeau Park, Belfast, on 18 March 1972.**

> I have reached the stage where I no longer have any compassion for any nationalist, man, woman, or child. After years of destruction, murder, discrimination, I have been driven against my better feelings to the decision — it's them or us. What I want to know is this, where the hell are the MEN of our community? Have they any pride? Have they any guts? Why are they not organized in, not defence, but commando groups? Why have they not started to hit back in the only way these nationalist bastards understand? That is ruthless indiscriminate killing. . . . If I had a flame-thrower, I would roast the slimy excreta that pass for human beings. Also I'm sick and tired of you yellow backed Prods who are not even prepared to fight for your own street, let alone your own loyalist people. When civil war breaks out, God forgive me, but I hope it's soon, I at least, will shoot you along with the Fenian scum.

The UDA joined the UVF and other Protestant para-militaries in mounting a campaign of blatantly sectarian murder. This sectarian violence reached its climax in the summer of 1972, and could be explained in part as a sort of violent mourning ritual among Protestants anticipating and then reacting to the British Government's dramatic closure in March of the Protestant unionist Parliament at Stormont.

The murder campaign continued on through the next decade, with other climaxes coming in late 1974, mid-1975, mid-1976, August 1979, and the summer of 1981. In 1980 the loyalists began to concentrate more on political assassinations, killing four prominent Irish nationalists; in January 1981 the UDA attempted to murder Bernadette Devlin McAliskey. In late 1982 a fresh wave of random sectarian killings of Catholics was cut short when Lennie Murphy, former leader of the Shankill Butchers, who were suspected of engineering most of the murders, was killed by the Provisional IRA. But back in 1972, when this kind of murder campaign began, the closure of the Protestant Parliament had been a major motive for Lennie Murphy and others.

The decision to close the Parliament at Stormont, from which the Protestant Unionist Party had ruled Northern Ireland for fifty years, was taken by Heath himself, very likely as a result of the general reaction to internment and the Bloody Sunday atrocity. Unionist rule was finished in Northern Ireland.

Soldiers of the British Army, given Catholic hatred and Protestant anger and contempt, began to see that they

(Below) British troops and RUC men in a clash with Protestants at Dungiven, Co. Derry, in June 1971. The Reverend William McCrea, a supporter of the Rev. Ian Paisley, is at right.

were at the mercy of both communities: The peacekeepers patrolling the streets knew now that death could come from any quarter at any time.

But what caused grim satisfaction among Catholic paramilitaries and their sympathizers was the presence of the ancient adversary, again directly in charge of the suppression of Irishry in Ireland.

How fully fledged an antagonist the British Army was, was epitomized in exchanges reported by the photographer Clive Limpkin, chronicler of the Battle of the Bogside, who had returned to Derry at about this time:

> "Hey, mister, d'you want to photograph a dead fucker then? We've got a bastard through the head. We shot his fucking head off. Over here."
>
> The boy was leading me round to Columbcille Court when I saw the soldiers bringing him out on a stretcher. They carried him down an alley and through a burnt-out garage to an army ambulance.
>
> He was dead, covered with a blanket.
>
> The news spread amongst the crowd in Rossville Street.
>
> "What's going on, then?"
>
> "The lads have shot a bastard."
>
> "Right through the chest."
>
> "No, it was the head. They shot his fucking head off. That'll teach the fucking bastard."
>
> A boy held out a cap badge to me. "D' you want to buy his cap badge, mister?"
>
> "D'you want to photograph his brains, then? All over the fucking pavement then?"
>
> The crowd grew as the news spread. They formed a line parallel with the troops blocking the mouth of Rossville Street.
>
> And the chanting began.
>
> > "If you kill a British soldier, clap your hands,
> > If you kill a British soldier, clap your hands,
> > If you kill a British soldier, kill a British soldier,
> > If you kill a British soldier, clap your hands."
>
> It was the younger ones singing, the older ones craned forward to watch the tension.
>
> > "We shot him through the head,
> > We shot him through the head,
> > Eee aye addio,
> > We shot him through the head."
>
> "Hey, Tarmmy, was he a friend of yours then? Was he then, Tarmmy?"

(Right) Youths chasing British soldiers at Free Derry wall following British Army killings of Seamus Cusack and Desmond Beattie in July 1971.

(Left) A British soldier in position opposite Stormont on the opening day of Whitelaw's Northern Ireland Regional Assembly: 31 July 1973.

6
Assembling a Government

WILLIAM WHITELAW was appointed by the British Prime Minister Edward Heath as minister plenipotentiary or Secretary of State for Northern Ireland, and Direct Rule by the British Government was inaugurated. Whitelaw, seeking to re-establish Britain's position as intermediary, held a kind of open house for Catholic and Protestant politicians. More than that, he showed himself willing to meet both Protestant and Catholic paramilitaries. Members of the UDA went to see him at Stormont — embarrassing the British Government by wearing face masks. The chief troublemakers on the Catholic side were the leaders of the Provisional IRA. Whitelaw seemed to have had in mind a political initiative in Northern Ireland, and he apparently wanted the cooperation of the two-and-a-half year old Provisional organization in, as he thought, creating the right climate for such an initiative. His objective was to restore local government to Northern Ireland, with fairer treatment for Catholics. What the Provisionals wanted from Whitelaw included an immediate end to internment, amnesty for prisoners in Northern Ireland and British jails because of the conflict, a cessation of hostilities by British troops. What the Provos wanted most of all was a declaration by the British Government that it was for

the people of Ireland as a whole to decide the future of Ireland as a whole, and a promise that the British would withdraw all their troops from Ireland within two-and-a-half years.

A truce was negotiated between the British and the IRA. And in a secret meeting in July 1972 in Chelsea, London, Whitelaw and his negotiators agreed to consider the Provos' points, and to deal with the Protestant militants — as the IRA had also asked. Whitelaw agreed to hold further talks.

But two days later the British Army interfered in a matter of moving dispossessed Catholics into some homes allocated to them by the local housing authority in Lenadoon Estate on the western edge of Andersonstown in Belfast, homes which had been abandoned by Protestants; the Army intervened on the side of armed paramilitary Protestants to prevent the Catholics from moving in.

The Army used CS gas, rubber bullets and a water cannon against the Catholics. They smashed a Saracen armoured car into a furniture van. It was difficult to say whether this was done under British Government orders or whether, as was more likely, the Army was behaving like a loose cannon on the deck of British policy, as it had done before and would do again.

The Provisionals tried to get Whitelaw to intervene, to no avail. They said the British, by letting their Army do this, had violated the truce, and they resumed their campaign of violence.

Whitelaw had made a practical decision in agreeing to the negotiations with the Provos in the first place: Had any

(Above)   Protestant rally at the Parliament building at Stormont the day the Northern Ireland Assembly was prorogued: 23 May 1972.

(Right)   Lenadoon estate in Belfast, July 1972. Troops fire rubber bullets at Catholics trying to move into houses assigned to them after Protestants had moved out.

Over the years people have been accustomed to hearing the gunmen and bombers of the Provisional IRA described as "men of violence," as though that rather than their political aims were the sole ground of objection to them.

Only now and then a naive voice like that of the child who piped up about the Emperor's New Clothes has ventured to ask what the British soldiery — let alone the Protestant paramilitaries — are to be described as, other than "men of violence."

If they are not trained in acts of violence, if they are not conditioned to act with violence whenever violence is advantageous, their existence is a fraud and the taxpayers are wasting good money on their training.

A soldier's training does not end with training simply in the ability to shoot straight or to operate a tank. If he is to be an efficient soldier he has to be conditioned to react quickly in the use of these skills; in other words to think and act violently.

Claud Cockburn

(Left)   Sean Mac Stiofain, pictured in 1972 when he was Chief of Staff of the Provisional IRA.

British colonial wars ever been ended without dealing directly with the military or guerrilla forces involved? Whitelaw had briefly put aside the traditional British posture of refusing to allow men "to shoot or bomb their way to the negotiating table," a posture that overlooked the fact that the Northern Ireland State had been founded on Protestant Irish threats of violence and that overlooked also the activities of the heavily armed men of violence of the British military forces. Whitelaw had pleaded for the IRA's co-operation. But in the final analysis he and his negotiators seemed to view the Provos as unworthy adversaries, and seemed to dismiss their complaints about the Lenadoon situation with contempt, allowing the ceasefire to become a dead letter.

Whitelaw's reversion to a kind of hardline colonialist view of the Provisional IRA found an answer in an IRA now under the hardline leadership of Seán Mac Stiofain, the English-born chief of staff. Mac Stiofain had done time in English prisons with guerrilla fighters who had learned their trade in the hard school of colonial warfare under the tutorship of brutal British adversaries in places like Cyprus and Aden. Mac Stiofain's IRA was not the hit-and-miss outfit of the 40s and 50s but a kind of Irgun (also a British creation) which struck with a ferocity that alarmed even IRA men of the older school—whose fighting had lacked a certain ruthlessness. The new Provos mounted a bombing campaign that shocked not only the Protestant but the Catholic people of

(Above) Men collecting bits of bodies in polythene bags after the killings on Bloody Friday: 21 July 1972.

Northern Ireland generally. The culmination came on Friday, July 21, 1972, only days after the breakdown of the truce, when the Belfast IRA exploded some twenty-two bombs in the centre of Belfast within a period of an hour and a quarter, killing eleven people and maiming and injuring one hundred thirty others. Whitelaw said publicly that he would never again negotiate with the IRA, and was heard to lament ever afterward that he had decided to sit at the table with them in the first place.

The evening of the Belfast bombings, there were television pictures of the carnage in the city centre: the day came to be called Bloody Friday. One piece of footage showed what was left of a human body being scooped like offal from in front of a bus terminal. Later an ex-Provo, Maria Maguire, wrote:

I . . . tried to find out just what had gone wrong on Bloody Friday. What I had read in the press was that the Belfast Provisionals claimed to have given at least an hour's warning for each bomb, but these warnings had not been followed up.

But I found it impossible to believe that no one in the Belfast leadership had realized how difficult it would be for the police and Army to act on twenty or more warnings received in the space of an hour.

All along we [the Provisionals] had known that there were risks of civilian casualties due to misunderstandings of our warnings and delays in acting on them.

I could not avoid the conclusion that the probability of civilian casualties had been accepted, perhaps even planned. Whenever such casualties had occurred before, there had always been the pressure of events to take my mind off them. But now, almost for the first time, I wondered about the crippled and the widowed and the lives that had been changed forever . . .

This came from a woman who though she had left the Provos was still sympathetic to their ideals; it was perhaps small wonder that Protestant reaction was strong.

The Protestant campaign of sectarian murder and torture that began in earnest that summer was in part a retaliation against the Provos. They, in turn, eventually began a counter-campaign of murdering innocent Protestants, replying to Protestant sectarian assassinations with killings of their own — though not, it seems, with any policy of torture.

The Protestant paramilitary interrogators seem to have taken their lead from the Army and RUC. Some of these freelance interrogators, who did their "rompering" of Catholics in private "romper rooms" hidden away in remote houses in the Protestant ghettoes, sought, like the Army and RUC to use torture to get information and "confessions."

The Protestant torturers were also like the British interrogators in that they seemed to want to make their violence known, so as to intimidate Catholics generally. An evident case in point was the Protestant torturing of a man named Thomas Madden, described as an inoffensive bachelor, who was employed as a night watchman:

Madden was stabbed approximately one hundred and fifty times. A detective said of these wounds at the time: "I stopped counting after fifty — there were so many." These wounds covered every part of the body including the scalp, the face, the arms, the legs, and the torso. They would appear to have been administered by a nine-inch double blade, in the nature of small nicks . . . to cause pain to the victim, not to kill him. . . . Possibly he was suspended in a slowly tightening noose that gradually strangled him while his assailants chipped away at his body with a knife like a sculptor at a block of stone . . .

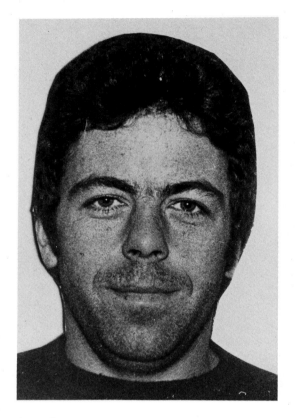

(Above) Lennie Murphy, a UVF man from the Shankill Road area of Belfast, credited with a leading role in the torture killings of Catholics in the early 70s and with being leader of the Shankill Butchers' murder gang of the mid-70s. He was himself killed by the IRA on 17 November 1982.

(Right) Protestant youth guarded by other Protestants, members of the Ulster Defence Association, strapped to a lamppost in the Shankill Road, Belfast in July 1972.

As (Jack) Holland records... Paddy Wilson, a popular Catholic politician, was found with over thirty stab wounds and his throat cut; his Protestant secretary, Irene Andrews, was murdered equally brutally; and six years later, John White, a UDA killer, was convicted and sentenced for these murders. Distinctions are odious, but it is only fair to observe that the bitterest critics of the IRA have never accused them of the same element of sadism in their killings.

Grattan Freyer

While Whitelaw was working out his political initiative, the British Army was working the streets, and *its* interrogators and psycho-political technicians continued working over suspects in secret.

But within a year or so Whitelaw's political labours produced agreement on the structure of an assembly in which Protestant unionist politicians would share power with Catholic moderates in a government representing both major communities in Northern Ireland. The British saw the new Assembly as a vehicle in which Protestants and Catholics could learn to live together in a peaceful British Northern Ireland dominated by political cooperation.

It was a structure which commended itself to moderates on the ground and liberals everywhere; the plan might have worked in 1969 or 1970 or even in early 1971, before Britain had become deeply involved in the conflict. It would not work now.

The plan was submitted to its moderate signatories at Sunningdale in December 1973. It provided that Catholic politicians would hold five of the eleven ministerial portfolios, and included a thirty-two county Council of Ireland dimension.

Brian Faulkner — the hardline Stormont Prime Minister who had insisted on the policy of internment which led to such disaster — now a new-minted Protestant moderate, was chosen as Chief Executive; the SDLP's Gerry Fitt was chosen Deputy Chief Executive; and the principal begetter of these happy new arrangements, the brilliant Catholic parliamentarian John Hume, was made Minister for Commerce. For the first time in the history of the Northern Ireland state, Catholics had a real voice in the administration.

But there was a ghost at this feast of political amity.

(Above) British soldier taking cover behind armoured car during gun battle with IRA men in July 1972.

(Left)   William Whitelaw, Secretary of State for Northern Ireland, with party leaders Brian Faulkner (Unionist), Oliver Napier (Alliance) and Gerry Fitt (SDLP), following talks in 1973 on Whitelaw's Assembly and the formation of his power sharing executive.

(Left) Protestant women in East Belfast celebrate the fall of the power sharing executive at the end of May 1974.

7
Abandoning a Government

THOSE MEN "who had been causing all the trouble," the militants of the IRA and of the Protestant political and paramilitary right-wing, were not there at Sunningdale to celebrate with Faulkner, Fitt, Hume, their moderate colleagues and the heads of the British and Irish Governments. Protestant politicians like William Craig, Harry West and Ian Paisley were excluded because of their hardline opposition to the new arrangements. The paramilitaries had never been consulted about them.

On January 1, 1974, the Assembly became the legal government of Northern Ireland. But by the end of May it was just as dead as the old Stormont regime it had been meant to supplant.

Heath's government had been brought down in the February 1974 elections and replaced by a new Labour government under Harold Wilson.

A new Northern Ireland Secretary of State, Merlyn Rees, was sent by Wilson to sort out the native tribes across the water. Wilson and Rees pledged the Assembly their full support.

But the Provos saw the Assembly and its power-sharing executive as yet another attempt to perpetuate British rule in Ireland. They continued to make trouble.

109

The UDA and UVF, along with hardline Protestant politicians, saw the arrangement with its Council of Ireland dimension as a Trojan horse within the Protestant citadel which when opened up would be found to contain advance men for a United Ireland.

In the British general election — despite their winning only a bare majority with the voters — eleven out of twelve Westminster MPs opposed to the Assembly were elected. Many Protestants saw the election to Westminster of the hardline unionists as a repudiation of the power-sharing regime.

On May 17, 1974, a series of car bombs were mysteriously exploded in Dublin and in Monaghan town, killing twenty-seven people outright. Three others died later from their injuries.

Some accounts attributed the attacks to Protestant paramilitaries. These groups were busily occupied at the time in organizing a general strike in Northern Ireland, and both the UDA and UVF flatly denied responsibility.

The conclusion others had arrived at was that the car bombings, which took more lives than had any incident in Northern Ireland, were the work of the SAS or other British Army agents, working undercover in the South.

Yet it was subsequently revealed that it was in fact members of the UVF and the UDA, in about equal numbers, who organized the car bombings in Dublin and Monaghan. They wanted to serve notice on the British as well as the Catholic Irish, North and South, that in the general strike in the North they meant business.

(Below) Merlyn Rees speaking at St. Anne's Cathedral in Belfast in March 1976, nine days after ending special category status in the prisons.

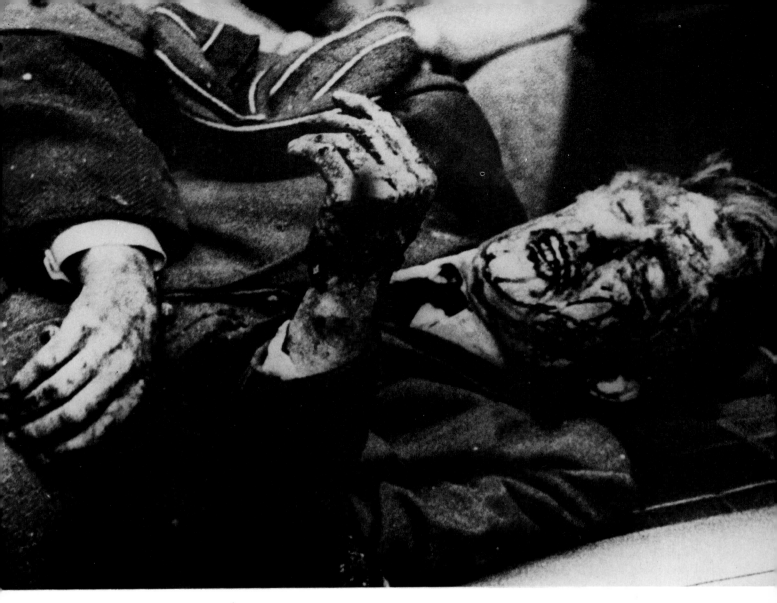

(Above) A victim of the loyalist car bombings in Dublin, 17 May 1974.

The UWC — the UDA- and UVF-supported Ulster Workers' Council — had warned in an advertisement a few days earlier that if the Assembly voted in support of Sunningdale there would be a general work stoppage. At a vote of confidence taken on May 14, Faulkner and his Catholic-Protestant coalition decisively won support for the Sunningdale arrangements.

The strike began next day, organized by Protestant workers and paramilitary leaders along with William Craig.

This revolution of Protestant working class extremists used various means, including intimidation at checkpoints in and around Belfast, to organize the stoppage. Days passed and the strike, which had key electrical power workers supporting it, became more and more widespread.

Yet nothing was done by Rees and the British Government to break the strike. Roy Mason, then Wilson's Defence Minister, issued what he called "a profound warning" to Wilson against the idea of trying to use the Army in breaking the strike. The British Army had passed the word that it was not going to break the strike. It didn't want a war on two fronts — against the IRA on one side and the Protestant paramilitaries on the other.

On May 23 several leaders of the Executive rushed off to London, hoping to get Harold Wilson to intervene with the Army. Wilson decided he couldn't do this. What he did instead was appear on television, bitterly criticizing the strikers, whom he had been privately calling "thugs" and "bullies," as "spongers" on British democracy. The speech was richly redolent of a British sense of injured majesty. The strikers wore sponges in their lapels next day, celebrating their facedown of Wilson and the British Government.

Finally the strikers threatened a complete shutdown, and on May 28 Faulkner and his moderate unionists resigned. The Assembly and its power-sharing executive were finished.

When the Army refused to act as an agent of British power in Northern Ireland, the British Government was rendered impotent. It did not govern during those days: the strikers governed. They held the power.

Many observers came to the conclusion that it was not constitutionality that determined legitimacy in Northern Ireland; it was *force majeure*.

Perhaps that was why British initiatives yielded in the end no response from the Catholic and Protestant Irish more audible than the echo of the sound George Bernard Shaw had heard from the Irish three quarters of a century earlier: "And all the while there goes on a horrible, senseless, mischievous laughter."

Shaw favoured Home Rule in 1912. His British friends commiserated with him: Once the protection of England was taken away, wasn't Shaw afraid of being persecuted in Ireland by Roman Catholics? Shaw said: "I would rather be burnt at the stake by Irish Catholics than protected by Englishmen."

The Sunningdale Assembly had discovered for itself the value of being under English protection.

The more this self-constituted "sovereign government" became involved as a managerial, penological and military participant in the conflict — and as an antagonist which could not even be relied on to control its own military wing — the less and less credible was its pose as disinterested intermediary between the warring tribes.

(Right)   Harry Murray, a principal leader of the UWC strike.

The conflict raged on. A Provisional campaign in the summer and autumn of 1974, culminating in the Birmingham bombings on 21 November, took the lives of dozens of wholly innocent people.

With Mac Stiofain now out of the way and others in control of the IRA, a peace initiative was set in motion through Provo co-operation with efforts made by Canon William Arlow and other Protestant clergymen of the Irish Council of Churches, who sought to get the IRA to the peace table.

The first face-to-face contact was at a secret meeting between the Churchmen and senior representatives of the Provisionals in Feakle, in County Clare in the Republic of Ireland, on December 10, 1974.

The Feakle meeting became public. Messages of support for the Feakle campaign poured in. Ian Paisley declared quite predictably that it was naive for the clergymen to hope that their "voices of sweet reasonableness" would deter "Satan's agents of death and destruction."

But on December 18, Merlyn Rees told the clergymen that if there was a genuine ceasefire the British Government would respond in a way that would gratify the Provisionals.

On December 30 the Provos announced that they were calling a ceasefire — it would endure, off and on, for nine months — as a direct result of "the courageous and positive action of the Church representatives whose approach, unlike others, was frank and constructive at all times." The Provos and the British met and negotiated.

On 1 May, 1975, elections for the Constitutional Convention were held. The Convention elections were boycotted by most Catholics, and hardline Protestant Irish politicians swept in by a heavy majority (forty-seven out of seventy-eight seats). These politicians issued their joint diktat: No Council of Ireland; no sharing of power with Catholics; the extermination of the Provos. It was the tiresome old message again.

But the Provos stayed quiet a while longer.

By confronting one violent power faction and then the other, by putting them in direct contact and then publicizing this effort, Canon Arlow and the Protestant clergymen of Feakle had done more to bring peace between the leading military factions than any other group had done or would do.

For the people of Northern Ireland, despite the fact that most Protestants regarded Arlow & Company as renegades, there had been a passage of relative peace. But in mid-1975 the Protestant sectarian murderers returned to the scene. In September the leaders of the IRA — some of whose members had been working freelance, or who had joined the new INLA (Irish National Liberation Army) because they didn't like truces — resumed their campaign.

During the truce the British security forces had been gathering information on the Provos.

(Above)   Daithi O Connail, a leader of the Provisionals, pictured in 1972.

(Above)   Canon William Arlow, Church of Ireland minister and then Assistant Secretary of the Irish Council of Churches, in December 1974.

(Right) British Prime Minister Harold Wilson with Merlyn Rees on the steps of Stormont Castle on 18 April 1974.

The British Government began to revert to a harder position. March 1, 1976, was arbitrarily chosen as the date ending the arrangement by which convicted political offenders were given political status in the prisons. (The British called it "special category" status.) This date marked the beginning of the Labour Government's "criminalization" policy which meant that subsequently convicted paramilitary suspects were henceforth to be treated as common criminals.

From now on all bets were off.

The criminalization policy, combined with the vicious behaviour of certain Catholic-hating prison warders or "screws," was to have violent repercussions in the blanket protest beginning later that year, in the "no wash" and "dirt" protests that began in 1978, in the "H-Blocks movement" — which used the H-shaped confinement blocks of the Maze prison at Long Kesh as the symbol of the repressive British jails — and in the hunger strike deaths of 1981.

"Pigs" (British Army Humber one-tonner armoured personnel carriers) and land rovers in Falls Road, in aftermath of violence in August 1976 on fifth anniversary of internment.

8
Beating the Terrorists

WITH THE RISE and sudden fall of the Assembly and power-sharing executive, with the abandonment of the Feakle peace, with the British Government's new criminalization policy, the career of the Northern Ireland conflict had left a kind of adolescence and had settled into a hard maturity. The behaviour of the three major antagonists during the early career of the conflict had worked to set a fixed pattern for the later years. A kind of education in violence combined with deep-seated habits of distrust to ensure that the later years of the conflict would be marked by the deep scars of failure.

The exemplars of all this were the children of Northern Ireland, growing to adulthood under a regime of violence.

In August 1976 Catholics and Protestants of Northern Ireland watched as Merlyn Rees departed the scene, to be replaced as Northern Ireland Secretary by Roy Mason.

James Callaghan, "the Catholics' friend," had been chosen to replace Harold Wilson as Prime Minister.

Peter Taylor later wrote:

> Callaghan sent Mason to Northern Ireland because he wanted a clear, unequivocal line to be taken, the priority being the defeat of terrorism, not

117

further attempts to shuffle the well-thumbed political cards. Mason was the man for the job. It was an easy move for him to make, from one set of generals to another, from Minister of Defence to Secretary of State for Northern Ireland. Roy Mason felt at home with the military: one of his colleagues said that he greeted a man with a uniform like a long-lost brother . . .

To the media, the tough pipe-smoking Minister who marched round the province in a safari suit epitomized the government's determination to defeat terrorism. It was exactly what Jim Callaghan wanted, not least to reassure the Ulster Unionist MPs at Westminster whose support he needed to maintain his slender majority in the House of Commons . . .

Roy Mason's style and approach to the Irish problem were very different from those of his predecessor. Rees was a conciliator, a listener, a man of compromise, which some saw as indecision. Mason knew what he wanted, gave orders and expected them to be obeyed. Some called it arrogance. Rees devoured volumes of Irish history and understood the nuances of Irish politics. Mason had no time for history; security concerned the present not the past. Results were what mattered. The new Secretary of State was a natural partner for the new Chief Constable . . .

(Above) RUC Chief Constable Kenneth Newman, pictured in 1978. Newman was later knighted for his services to the Crown while in Northern Ireland.

The new RUC chief constable's name was Kenneth Newman. With Newman's help, Mason embarked on the most determined programme of interrogatory torture since the early days of internment. This time it was better targeted, however. They were not operating a dragnet—though they had their moments. Their operations were directed principally at the Provos and the nascent INLA and those closely associated with Catholic paramilitarism. When standard interrogatory measures failed to yield material the police interrogators wanted, or thought they could get, they turned to the brutal methods which Mason and Newman had made it clear — by their nods and winks and their enthusiasm about results — were quite acceptable when other methods had failed. The locus of most of this activity was Castlereagh Interrogation Centre.

What had become apparent during the successive years of British direct rule was that, in line with Mason's "get tough" policy, the British were maintaining and cultivating in Northern Ireland a violence establishment. In Northern Ireland the chief motive for doing or avoiding doing anything was the threat of force, including violent physical force. If people did not refrain from activities forbidden by those in power, they knew that the authorities would impose their will by guns and other explosive and coercive machines. In the prisons they would use torture if they chose to. Clearly now, in Northern Ireland, relationships were based nakedly on power on either side: on the use and threat of violence.

The British presence itself had made Northern Ireland a militarized society. To working-class Catholics at least the real basis for British legitimacy was obvious. British soldiers and police and war machines were omnipresent.

Under a regime of violence, attempts at parliamentary

The end of the power-sharing illusion; Provo persistence; torture in Castlereagh; degradation in the H-Blocks: all these served to stiffen the will of the Catholic community once again. But more than these and most of all it was the activity of the SAS which fuelled emotions through 1978.

In what was probably an attempt to deliver the coup de grace the Labour government gave the SAS licence to kill: summary execution of suspected Republicans. Ten people were executed in this way between December 1977 and November 1978. Colm McNutt from the Creggan, aged 18, an IRSP member, was shot dead by SAS men in plain clothes in a car park in William Street on 12 December. Paul Duffy, 20, a Provo, was ambushed and shot dead on 26 February near his home at Ardboe, County Tyrone. Denis Heaney [of Derry] was killed on 10 June. Three Ardoyne Provos, Jim Mulvenna, Denis Brown and Jackie Mealey were ambushed and killed while on the way, unarmed, to plant a bomb at a GPO depot in North Belfast on 21 June. Mealey had sixty-three bullet wounds; he was literally shot to pieces. A passing Protestant, Billy Hanna, was shot dead for good measure. John Boyle, 16, was shot dead on 11 July by an SAS unit waiting in ambush for a Provo unit which never arrived. James Taylor, a Protestant wildfowler, was shot dead near the shore of Lough Neagh on 30 September. Paddy Duffy, 50, who, acting as a messenger for the Provos, approached a cupboard which contained guns in a derelict house in Maureen Avenue in the Bogside on 25 November was shot from behind by SAS men hiding in an alcove across the room and using SLRs. There were eighteen bullet wounds in his body. The SLR can kill at a thousand yards . . .

Eamonn McCann

(Bottom) Roy Mason reviewing troops of the Royal Marine Commando in late 1976.

(Left) Scene on Finaghy Road in Belfast where the three Maguire children were struck by the van in August 1976.

(Below) The body of one of the Maguire children is carried to a hearse at the children's funeral.

politics had to be a charade. There could be no peace until the war, such as it was, was ended. Mason's way of peace, which in truth commended itself to most Protestants, was ruthless repression of terrorist suspects and of those who sympathized with them. As the counter-terror extended itself to the most nationalist-minded young males (and females) in certain districts, the IRA gained new recruits.

Mason's approach was not one likely to draw approval from civil libertarians. Yet just after coming to office, Mason found support in a totally unexpected quarter.

In August 1976, British troops in West Belfast killed an IRA man driving a van they were pursuing. The van, now totally out of control, killed three children of a Catholic family named Maguire. One of the children's aunts was a

capable young secretary named Mairead Corrigan. Together with a caustic sympathizer named Betty Williams, she promptly formed an organization called the Peace Women. They were joined by a young journalist, Ciaran McKeown, who was to become their regular spokesman and publicist.

Huge crowds of Catholic and Protestant women tumbled into the streets in enthusiastic response. They would meet across the sectarian divide, they said, and thereby put an end to the conflict. The movement drew international media attention. The women would, they said, achieve peace in Northern Ireland. They became the Peace People. There were

(Below) **Supporters of the Peace Women at the August 1976 Ormeau Park rally.**

(Above) The Peace Women, led by Betty Williams and Mairead Corrigan (holding telegrams), on a march to Ormeau Park in Belfast in August 1976.

monster rallies. The rallies of August continued into September, October and November. But there was a falling off in the numbers of people attending.

Now that the great enthusiasm of the rallies was over, the Peace People went rapidly into decline.

Why?

Among other things they had overlooked was the presence of a third party to the conflict. They had not acknowledged that Britain was an antagonist. They had focused rather on the tiresome old notion that the trouble lay essentially in Protestant and Catholic prejudice.

What the Peace People seemed to want was love and friendship across the board. But they were trying to effect these under a double disadvantage. In a regime of violence they had no power of their own. Nor did they have a practical political programme that would give them leverage with the power-obsessed physical force men dominating the scene: the Catholic and Protestant paramilitaries; the British Army and the police and UDR; and now — nicely personified in Roy Mason himself — the British Government as well.

By the time they received the Nobel Prize for Peace, the Peace Women no longer even appeared to have a significant role.

In the end, in this context of violence, events wrote the authors out of their own script. The year of the great Peace People rallies, 1976, saw twenty sectarian assassinations in its final month.

(Left)   Scene at a Belfast riot in 1977. Man lying injured on pavement is a British soldier.

Roy Mason, who as Northern Ireland Secretary was perhaps the Peace People's chief beneficiary, set out to tackle the job of "beating the terrorists." He made "criminalization" work, but at a price.

There was no question about the effectiveness of Mason's campaigns and about the sharp deterioration under Mason in the situation in the jails and concrete prison blocks. At Her Majesty's Prison The Maze — located on the site of an abandoned airstrip at a place not far from Belfast called Long Kesh — the prisoners embarked on a blanket protest and then later on the "no wash" and "dirt" protests. The blanket protest would last for five years.

As a result of the edict issued by Mason's predecessor Rees, all prisoners convicted of the use of violence for political purposes after March 1, 1976, were to be denied category (i.e., political or prisoner-of-war) status. The new prisoners didn't want to wear the British prison uniforms that were intended to mark them as common criminals.

In late 1976, after Mason had arrived on the scene, a young Provo named Ciaran Nugent who had been sentenced for hijacking a van, and hijacking it after the magical March date, turned up at Long Kesh.

Nugent decided not to put on the criminal uniform: "They would have to nail the clothes to my back," he said, if they

(Right)   Ciaran Nugent, who in late 1976 was the first man on the blanket protest at the Maze prison at Long Kesh, at a press conference after his release in May 1979, nearly three years later.

(Above) Prisoner on blanket protest in excrement-covered cell: He has been identified as Sean McKenna, the man later saved from death when the first group of hunger strikers called off their strike in December 1980.

(Left) Still life with rosary: a Catholic protester's cell in March 1979 at Long Kesh during the "dirt" protest.

wanted to force him to wear it. Instead of the uniform, he wore a prison-issue blanket. Other prisoners followed suit. Thus began the blanket protest.

In March 1978 came the "no wash" protest, after the warders began forcing some Provo and INLA prisoners to dry themselves with a scanty towel in front of jeering "screws" after their weekly bath. The prisoners refused to bathe at all. So they were beaten nearly senseless and dragged off to tubs and forced under often scalding showers.

Some time later, as a consequence of the continuing harassment, came the "dirt" protest. According to some accounts what happened was that the warders began kicking over the prisoners' chamber pots and slopping the contents against the prison floors. To prevent this the prisoners began throwing their slops out the window. The warders sealed the windows. So the prisoners began to daub the faeces on the walls to get them off the floors where they slept. This protest, like the blanket and no-wash protests, became a ritual with hundreds of the prisoners, which they were determined to continue until some basic demands of theirs were met, the primary and bottom line demands then being the right to wear their own clothes and the right not to do prison — i.e., criminals' — work.

The various protests in their earlier days were seen by the prisoners, too, as a way of highlighting and publicizing the conditions under which they were daily forced to live. They knew that the protests, singly or in combination, might lead to illness or disease in the prison, causing the deaths of some of them. In that sense these protests anticipated the hunger strikes of 1980 and 1981. The prisoners were willing to fight "criminalization" with their very lives.

127

9
Armed Impotence

IN MAY 1979 Margaret Thatcher became Conservative Party Prime Minister and Humphrey Atkins her Secretary of State for Northern Ireland. Thatcher maintained the "criminalization" policy. "A crime is a crime is a crime," would come to be a favourite phrase with her.

There was a personal factor which may have weighed heavily in Margaret Thatcher's rigid posture: her intimate friend and political mentor, the outspoken Airey Neave. A hero and planner of escapes from German prisoner-of-war camps during World War II, he had been appointed Shadow Secretary of State for Northern Ireland. Neave, who was Thatcher's choice as Mason's replacement should she win the 1979 election, had in the years prior to the election been promising to take a very hard line.

Leaders of the Provisional IRA seemed delighted at the prospect of Airey Neave as Northern Ireland Secretary of State, feeling that the tough policies he promised would create such a reign of terror that a British withdrawal of troops might become urgently necessary just to stabilize the Northern Ireland situation.

But Neave's promises made him a target for another Catholic paramilitary group: the INLA or Irish National Liberation Army. It was a new organization, the military arm of the IRSP (the Irish Republican Socialist Party)

(Above) Thatcher pictured with Airey Neave in June 1978 when she was opposition leader at Westminster and Neave was her spokesman on Northern Ireland.

which had broken away from the Official IRA because leaders of the Officials had decided to turn away from violent involvement in the conflict and to go political. On March 31, 1979, apparently motivated by desire for a "stroke," a *coup d'théatre*, the INLA struck a savage blow against the British Parliament and Mrs. Thatcher. Using a delayed action bomb, they blew up Airey Neave in his car as he drove out from an underground car park at the House of Commons.

The Provos took some five months to even the score with the INLA, getting their own "prestige target" with the remote control bomb killing of Lord Louis Mountbatten, two members of his family and a young friend. Mountbatten, an uncle of Prince Philip, the Queen's husband, was an admired military leader during World War II. He was killed in the Republic, near his holiday home in County Sligo, in late August, 1979.

On the same day as the Mountbatten murders the Provisional IRA killed eighteen British soldiers by remote control bombs at Warrenpoint, County Down. The IRA, claiming responsibility for both actions, said that the "execution" of Mountbatten was a "discriminate operation to bring to the attention of the English people the continuing occupation of our country."

It was during the first months of the Thatcher/Atkins period, during which nothing had changed in the H-Blocks,

(Below) **The remains of the body of Lord Mountbatten being carried from the harbour near Sligo where his boat was blown up on 27 August 1979.**

that the Mountbatten and Warrenpoint killings took place. Atkins, who was no Roy Mason or Airey Neave, commended himself to some in Northern Ireland as an intelligence gatherer. To most he was a kind of living symbol of British indifference to Northern Ireland, a man innocent of any real idea of what the conflict was about or how to resolve it.

Under direct pressure from Margaret Thatcher, Humphrey Atkins sought a series of consultations with the various political parties in Northern Ireland. Atkins' consultations were timed to coincide with the American presidential primary campaign season, in the cynical awareness that they would serve to quiet Senator Edward Kennedy who had frequently been an outspoken critic of British policy in Northern Ireland.

During these discussions the violence in the six counties raged unabated. Apart from hypocrisy, there was the old attitude of negligent indifference. To some Atkins personally epitomized this British attitude, and the habit of playing for time in the hope that the bothersome violence would somehow "sort itself out" or go away.

Not surprisingly, Atkins' talks delivered only the bare pretence of a proposal for devolved government, principally because the politicians of the SDLP — John Hume had taken over the leadership — told Atkins that they would not involve themselves in any further pretext of talks unless a solid Irish dimension and Catholic power-sharing were on the table.

(Below) Scene of the IRA bomb explosion on 27 August 1979 at Warrenpoint, Co. Down, which killed 18 soldiers.

(Above) Two days after the Mountbatten and Warrenpoint killings, Margaret Thatcher was in Belfast with Timothy Creasy, the then British Army commander in Northern Ireland; in the middle is Humphrey Atkins. So shaky was British Army morale after Warrenpoint that it was said that if Thatcher hadn't come to visit the Army, there wouldn't have been any Army left to visit in Northern Ireland.

(Left) Rev. Ian Paisley addressing a huge crowd of loyalists in workers' rally at Victoria Park, Belfast, early in the conflict: in September 1971.

(Below) Ten years later, in March 1981, Paisley leads a small crowd of faithful supporters — to the "monster rally" at Stormont at the conclusion of his "Carson trail" caper. The paradox was that as the crowds responding to Paisley's incitements to violence dwindled, support for him and his Democratic Unionist Party increased.

Ian Paisley was leader of the only major unionist political faction (the increasingly powerful DUP) that bothered attending Atkins' conferences. Paisley had made it perfectly clear from the outset that neither an Irish dimension nor power-sharing would be acceptable to "the good Protestant people of Ulster" he represented.

And indeed Paisley now represented a great many of them. He had regained prominence by winning some 170,000 first preference votes in the European parliamentary elections of June 1979, three months after the murder of Airey Neave. Protestants who didn't like Paisley's ranting bigotry voted for him — "in a cowardly way," as one of them put it — as the sole sufficiently noisy custodian of the creaky shell of what was once Ulster unionism. Yet there was something else beginning to emerge in place of that unionism; and Paisley, willy-nilly, had become a standard bearer for that, too.

From late 1969, when Protestants found themselves in occasional confrontation with the British Army and, after the Army's intervention, even with their own police, the old Protestant suspicions of Britain's disloyalty began to resurface. After the startup of internment, and especially in 1972, a radical change began to occur in the outlook of Protestants, especially of the working class.

The unionist Stormont that had held them in thrall was now suddenly gone. With the mass protest rallies organized by William Craig, a new kind of Protestant politics began to emerge; it was a tougher politics and, in default of promised leadership from Protestant politicians like Craig and Harry West and Ian Paisley, it became an authentically working-class movement — just as agrarian Orangeism, begun as a movement of poor Protestant farmers, had been in 1795, before the wealthy manipulators got hold of it.

With the end of the old B-Specials and the advent of British Direct Rule, Protestants found themselves unable to deal with Catholics as they had become accustomed to dealing with them. There was a kind of castration effect, symbolized by the dismemberment of the Specials. And the UDR that replaced them was under British Army rather than loyalist control.

The new loyalism was quite independent of the old Unionist Party political plutocracy which had used the Stormont Parliament to feather its own nest of money and power interests, a party which, following the demise of the Stormont government, began immediately to sink in influence. The new loyalists began suddenly to query all this: to ask questions about the Unionist government that had ruled them for fifty years and then had suddenly been closed down. At the end Protestants had lost ultimate control of Northern Ireland.

So, while unionism began the slow burn-out that would end in the disintegration of the old landlord and industrialist unionism, a fired-up, paramilitarized working-class loyalism began to emerge uncertainly, and even bloodily, like a hard-born phoenix from the blackened unionist shell.

The new loyalism did of course maintain on the surface the tradition of loyalty to "the British Crown in Parliament." But the younger, street-wise Protestants soon came to define loyalism for all practical purposes as loyalty to themselves and their notions of how the six counties ought to be run. And they were not happy with some of the arrangements the Crown's Parliament was setting in motion in Northern Ireland.

It was not lost on the new loyalists that in the UWC strike they had faced down a British Government whose prescriptions for governance in Northern Ireland did not suit them. (Nor was it lost on observers that the Provos were sitting happily on the sidelines, cheering on the strikers, with bonfires blazing far into the night in West Belfast.)

Some of the UDA leaders regretted that they had not pushed their strike further. They had defeated the Assembly and its power-sharing executive. They might have gone on to use a continued strike to force the British government to set up a strong Protestant parliament at Stormont again.

(Right)   Queen Elizabeth meeting Northern Ireland children at Hillsborough, Co. Down, during her Silver Jubilee visit to Northern Ireland in August 1977.

This was perhaps the start of the UDA thinking that led three years later to their call, through their New Ulster Political Research Group (NUPRG), for an independent Northern Ireland.

This was not an unfamiliar idea.

Protestant thinking about Northern Ireland had always had two strains. First there was the unionist strain, which saw union with Britain as the safeguard of the Protestant people of Ireland — who since the 1920s had been heavily concentrated in the northeast of the six counties.*

This unionist school of thinking was proud of the British connection, and a large segment of it — represented today by Enoch Powell and James Molyneaux — wanted more and more integration with Britain.

Another strain of Protestant thinking stemmed from the proud sense of independence of colonial settlers. Whatever about the English or British connection, they would hold their own Protestant Israel, their Promised Land, against all comers.

For centuries these two traditions — of Britishness and of independence — had coexisted side by side. Through the fifty years of the Stormont regime most Protestants had remained British. Yet they had run things in Northern Ireland to suit themselves.

---

*Protestants were concentrated in the industrialized area around Belfast, in Antrim and in North Down and North Armagh. But Fermanagh, Tyrone, South Armagh, South Down, Derry City and most of County Derry continued to be majority Catholic areas.

From the time of the start of the conflict in 1968, and especially from the time of Direct Rule in 1972, Ian Paisley — more than any other political leader in Northern Ireland — had used the regime of violence itself, the weakness of Britain, British indifference and neglect, the uncertainty and instability of British policy: he had used all these factors against Molyneaux and Enoch Powell and his other British-lining adversaries. He could say: Look at them, kowtowing to Westminster: Ulster Protestants can stand on their own feet!

By 1977 the UDA was taking the same general line. There were complex reasons for this. With Mason suddenly on the scene, "security" (meaning defence against the IRA and INLA) seemed to be in good hands. The UDA and the UVF and other Protestant paramilitary organizations were irrelevant at a time when Westminster was hammering the Catholic paramilitaries. There seemed to be no point at the moment for a group which maintained itself by lashing out at innocent Catholics in response to Provo killings of soldiers and police. The Protestant population as a whole didn't condone these sectarian murders of innocent Catholics. And under Mason the soldiers and police were taking care of themselves.

What does a paramilitary group do when it is out of business as a fighting outfit? When the British and local "security forces" are doing their job for them? In the UDA's own metaphor, they wrap themselves into a tight little ball and wait for the tide to turn. They maintain a skeleton structure to protect the organization.

But in this inter-conflict period, they must maintain visibility, and must apply their energies to something. Therefore the political initiative. The leaders of the UDA knew that British policy was fundamentally unreliable. If their UDA had to stand for something other than a readiness to lash out at innocent Catholics in times of weak British government, politics might be the answer. Besides, in earlier years UDA men, like other Protestant paramilitaries, had found themselves brutally flailing away in a political vacuum. Maybe they could do something to fill that political vacuum, permanently.

In the long run, many of their more politically-minded people thought, the British were bound to abandon Northern Ireland to its own devices. The UDA had better be ready with some political alternative to continued British rule. That strain of independence thinking, always present in Irish settler Protestantism, was the kind of thinking they could build on. They didn't want to abandon the Union. But it was likely that at some point, from the British side, the Union would abandon them.

(Above) **The Pope on his visit to Ireland in September 1979.**

So — and paradoxically with the help of the Irish-born American lawyer Paul O'Dwyer, a veteran of Irish nationalist causes — they began to organize their thinking along the lines of a kind of American model independent Ulster, with a Bill of Rights that might attract the Catholic minority. And they developed a secular, anti-sectarian theme in their rhetoric, distancing them from Paisley. For many reasons, including rivalry for power, they wanted to make certain that they were not mistaken for Paisleyites. After all it was they, and not Paisley, who had made the 1974 UWC strike work. (Paisley had managed to absent himself in Canada while the strike had got uncertainly underway.) They had a claim to power — their latent military force — that Paisley lacked. He was merely a rhetorician of violence. They controlled instruments of violence.

When it was suggested in the spring and summer of 1979 that Pope John Paul II might visit Northern Ireland in September, Paisley raised a hue and cry, invoking the old Orange slogan, "No Pope here."

Yet the UDA, less interested in symbols, passed the word along to the Catholic bishops of Ireland that they would give no support to Paisley's threats: The Pope could visit any part of Ireland he wanted to without interference from them. (As it happened, the Mountbatten and Warrenpoint murders intervened in August, and the Catholic bishops found in the resultant spasm of emotion reason to advise the Pope against visiting Northern Ireland.)

Nor did the UDA dispatch its foot soldiers to swell the numbers at Paisley's "monster rally" at the conclusion of his "Carson Trail" in 1981, a rally which turned out a pitiful crowd of fewer than ten thousand marchers, mostly ageing fundamentalists.

The paradox was that while Paisley and his DUP, originally a poor farmers' party, were now getting votes (on a "cowardly" basis) from frightened Protestants of the middle class — and by dint of hard constituency work from the working class — this was taken by many as suggesting that Paisley controlled vast hosts of gunmen.

But there was little evidence, even in his Third Force campaign of late 1981, that Paisley controlled any paramilitary effectives, apart from a few already enrolled in the Crown forces — the UDR and the RUC and RUC reserve.

They marched by night, Paisley's fearsome legionnaires, not by day. The UDA, the most powerful of the Protestant paramilitary groups, had marched by day; and its leaders were increasingly doubtful allies of Paisleyism.

During the last years of the 1970s there had been a sharp fall-off in the UDA campaign of indiscriminate sectarian murder. Andy Tyrie, Supreme Commander of the UDA, whose name had been associated with UDA sectarian murder campaigns, seemed to be the man who had most to do with curtailing them. This changed UDA policy had been applied very specifically after the La Mon House Hotel bombing in February 1978, near Comber, County Down. There an explosive device, wired to two cans of petrol, was suspended outside a window of the hotel restaurant. The IRA bomb warning came much too late. Intended to destroy only the hotel proper, the bomb exploded prematurely, creating a fireball which rolled within seconds through the hotel's public rooms, killing twelve Protestants and injuring more than thirty others.

What was remarkable was that the UDA leaders had felt confident enough of control over their membership at that stage to publicly announce immediately after La Mon that there would be no retaliation against innocent Catholics for what had happened at the hotel.

In his book on the IRA, Tim Pat Coogan, editor of *The Irish Press*, wrote:

> One of the main architects of the UDA's shift in emphasis from the bullet and the knife to political activity is Andy Tyrie . . .
> At moments of crisis, such as in the aftermath of the La Mon bombing when he was beseiged by heated calls

(Above)   Andy Tyrie, Supreme Commander of the Ulster Defence Association, at UDA headquarters in Newtownards Road, Belfast, in May 1981.

140

for a resumption of the assassination campaign, he has been known to throw a list of top IRA men's names on to a table and with them a gun, saying "Those are the men you want, pick up the gun and I will give you as many more as you want to do the job — but there's no use shooting Catholics just for revenge."

The UDA in fact began to concentrate in the early 80s on shootings of admired Catholic nationalist leaders.

Still, these Protestant paramilitaries had come to take a less murderous line. Why, then, were the Provos and the INLA so intent on continuing a campaign of violence aimed at killing public figures, British soldiers, police and UDR men: a campaign that sometimes resulted in the deaths of innocents and always brought the Provos bad publicity?

At any given time the IRA and INLA mustered only three or four hundred armed active service volunteers (though there were several thousand in the support networks). On the other side there were some twenty-three thousand British soldiers, UDR and armed police. These, taken together with auxiliaries and armed Protestant loyalist paramilitaries, mustered a total of up to forty thousand. The IRA and INLA

(Below) Ruins of La Mon House Hotel, near Comber, Co. Down, after the explosion and fire in February 1978.

active service units were therefore outnumbered by something like a hundred to one on the ground in Northern Ireland. Yet they retained broad enough Catholic support to remain a major contributor to the violence.

Why this continued campaign, and why the support?

Was it because Catholics in Northern Ireland were faced with continued hostility and discrimination under British direct rule, and with more continual daily attentions from the "security forces"? "It's a police state," the Crossmaglen publican Paddy Short said: "We have no rights." Yet in essence the Republicans' reason for continuing the war was simply Britain's refusal to withdraw from Ireland.

It remained for Margaret Thatcher to enrage Catholics and deepen the polarization of the two communities in Northern Ireland by her attitude toward the hunger strikers.

The first major hunger strike in 1980 had nearly reached a fatal conclusion when, to save the life of one of their number, Seán McKenna, six men came off their strike. But Thatcher's government—more, it seems, because of her own personal feelings than of obstinacy on the part of prison governor Stanley Hilditch and his warders at Long Kesh—did nothing in response.

IRA and INLA prisoners felt that the British had betrayed an implied promise to meet their demands, and Bobby Sands, now commanding officer of the IRA men in the prison, announced that he was going to be the first volunteer on a new hunger strike. He was, and he began in March 1981.

During the early days of Sands' hunger strike, a Westminster paliamentary seat became vacant in the majority Catholic area of Fermanagh-South Tyrone. The leaders of the H-Blocks movement, now mobilized in support of Sands, suddenly came up with the idea of running him for the seat in the hope that the publicity thus generated would help force the British Government to meet Sands' and the other strikers' most basic demands: the right to wear their own clothes, the right to free association within the prison, and the right to reject what they considered demeaning forms of prison work.

A nationalist vote of over thirty thousand in these majority Catholic Counties brought Sands the seat. Many Catholics expected that this bloodless victory at the ballot box would encourage the British Government to meet the prisoners halfway. Instead they took the next opportunity to exclude all prisoners from candidacy for Westminster elections.

> *You cannot put a rope*
> *around the neck of an idea.*
> *You cannot put an idea*
> *against a barrack wall*
> *and riddle it with bullets.*
> *You cannot confine it*
> *in the strongest prison cell*
> *that your slaves could ever build.*
>
> *Bobby Sands, MP*
> *Lettering on wall*
> *Rockmore and Falls Roads*
> *Belfast*

(Right) Bobby Sands.

(Below)   Some 90,000 people marched in Bobby Sands' funeral procession, here seen enroute from Twinbrook estate in Belfast on 7 May, 1981.

(Above)   Funeral procession of Francis Hughes on 15 May 1981. Hughes was the second hunger striker to die. Marching behind his coffin is his 74-year old father Joe Hughes.

It's nice to be tough. But it would be better to be tough about other issues than this. There are special courts and special legislation, so why can't there be special prisoners?

Andy Tyrie

. . . It is evident that [Thatcher] really does take pleasure in displaying herself as standing firm against the dying men in Long Kesh. It is clear that as her troubles get worse and her critics more critical she has come obsessed with the notion of her own "toughness," as though toughness was somehow an end in itself.

Watching her behaviour in this matter one could incline to believe the theory of those who think that her emotional attitude to the North is really determined by her past emotional relationship to Airey Neave . . .

Claud Cockburn

Atkins, echoing Thatcher, delivered himself of by now well-rehearsed lines about the British Government refusing to give in to the prisoners' demands: conceding them would amount to admitting that the prisoners were political prisoners and not common criminals.

What was Bobby Sands' view? He was offering his life in protest against, as he said, the "barbarity . . . beatings and inhumanity" he'd experienced in the prison at Long Kesh, and for the freedom of Ireland from British control. He did not sound like a common criminal. In fact he conveyed an earnestness and charm, partly by what he had written, partly by accounts of how he had memorized the plot line of *Trinity* and shouted the story down the corridor of his cell block each night. "Geronimo" the other prisoners called him. He attracted an overwhelmingly favourable press, and became a kind of international media celebrity.

Various religious leaders pleaded with Sands to give up his fast. Two other Provo hunger strikers, Francis Hughes and Raymond McCreesh — and an INLA man, Patsy O'Hara — were already in serious condition. The world waited and watched. It was, the journalist Claud Cockburn said, "precisely because of the peculiar personality of Mrs. Thatcher [that] the callousness and stupidity of Westminster have in this case been spectacularly illuminated."

All four died — and they were the first of ten who would die. The other six were Joe McDonnell, Martin Hurson, Kevin Lynch, Kieran Doherty, Thomas McElwee and Micky Devine. Editors of newspapers throughout the world, responding to a *Sunday Times* questionnaire, sided by more than seven to one with the IRA's objectives of British withdrawal and Irish unification as against a continued British presence in Northern Ireland.

When Atkins was finally removed from office in late 1981, polarization between the two Irish antagonists was deeper than it had been since 1972. Supporters of Ronald Reagan, during the 1980 American presidential election campaign, had attacked the Carter administration's posture on international intervention as "armed impotence." Would the Thatcher government's contribution to the Northern Ireland problem be summarized for history in some such phrase?

In late 1981 James Prior, because of his disagreements with Thatcher's economic policies and methods, was exiled in effect from British mainstream politics by being demoted to the position of Northern Ireland Secretary. For Prior, an ambitious man much talked of as a future leader of the Conservative Party, it seemed an opportunity.

Within two weeks of his taking office, the seven months' hunger strike came to an end. There was relative peace in the prisons when most of what the hunger strikers had wanted was granted to their fellow prisoners. When Prior first came, he seemed to believe that the Northern Ireland problem would have to be internationalized before any real solution could be found — which showed at least a decent diffidence about the ability of the British to solve a problem to which they were so profound a contributor. Yet Prior's first major political move was to offer a governmental plan that was fully as much of a charade as those of his immediate predecessors.

Prior's plan, which took the form of a consultative Assembly, was doomed from the start. Only Paisley's Democratic Unionist Party and the minor Alliance Party supported it. The Official Unionists and their British Tory allies fought against the Assembly bill in the Westminster Parliament. Thatcher, with her Falklands victory behind her, did little to discourage MPs who used the bill to attack Prior. Thatcher eventually let the bill pass. There was an election, and the Official Unionists, the largest of the unionist parties, felt vindicated when to Prior's evident dismay Provisional Sinn Fein, under Gerry Adams' leadership, won six of the Assembly seats and ten per cent of the votes: some *thirty-five* per cent of the identifiably Catholic votes. Prior was shocked. But John Hume's anti-violence SDLP (the "stoop down low party" of Republican gibes), which had been willing to work within a British constitutional context, had been betrayed once again by the British. Hume was damaged as much by Prior's pallid initiative as he had been by Thatcher's hot-faced intransigence during the hunger strike, and the SDLP was forced in the circumstances to boycott the Assembly along with Sinn Fein. Britain had made a mess of yet another initiative, a mess that would take awhile to clear away. While in the Assembly Paisley was more or less on his best behaviour, other members of what was now only a puppet and pretend parliament made capital use of the forum to put Prior on the defensive. An Irish journalist, accustomed to South Dublin where people generally not only spoke no evil of Britain but tried to think no evil, came to Belfast to report some of the deliberations of this almost wholly Protestant body, and was astonished at the level of anti-British invective: bitter criticism of the British Government and Prior, complaints about "security" and powerlessness and various other recriminations were hurled across the floor of the Assembly chamber by the "loyalist British" Protestant members. The only kind of news that brought real cheers from the floor was the word from Prior that "clandestine" operations were getting results, meaning unarmed Catholic paramilitary suspects (and innocent Catholics) were now being shot on sight by Prior's police and Army. These summary executions were about as "clandestine" as a flashing red light. But most of the Protestant unionist Assembly members seemed mollified for the moment.

Through the first half of 1983 it became increasingly clear that Thatcher, Prior and the Protestant unionist politicians—unwilling to give an inch to the moderate nationalists of the SDLP—were continuing to aid and abet the political rise of the militant Provos. Provisional Sinn Fein's success in the 1982 Assembly elections was surpassed by their achievement in the June 1983 Westminster parliamentary elections. Sinn Fein increased its vote to 103,000—a stunning *forty-three* percent of the Northern Irish Catholics who voted. This new success came despite the fact that Sinn Fein's military wing, the Provisional IRA, was unrelentingly

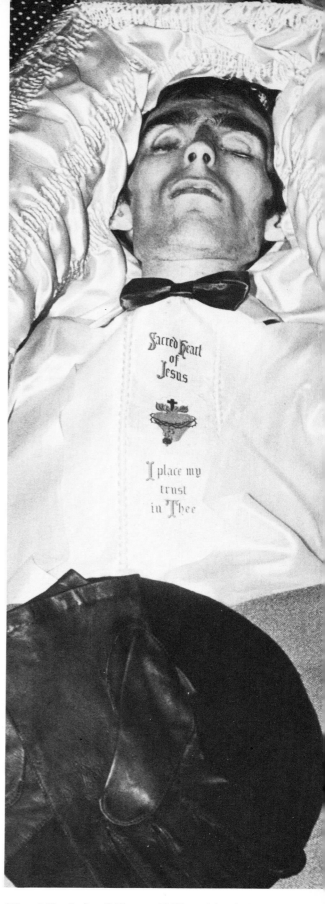

(Above) **The body of Thomas McElwee lying in his coffin.**

146

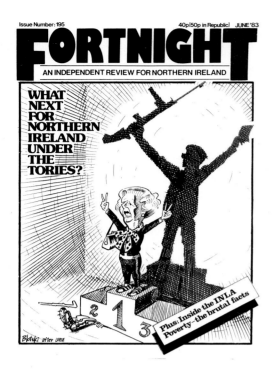

FORTNIGHT magazine cover:
June 1983 post-election issue

(Above) James Prior, British Secretary of State for Northern Ireland from September 1981.

and at times nastily active during the Westminster election campaign. The Provos' success at the ballot box — which began with Bobby Sands' H-Block election victory and was inspired by memories of the ten hunger strikers — created the pressure that forced the SDLP and the three major Southern Irish political parties (Fianna Fail, Fine Gael and Labour) to finally get down to work, in what was called the New Ireland Forum, to produce a detailed blueprint for a thirty-two county Ireland, in which the Protestant and Catholic Irish might live together amicably: something that has proved impossible under British rule. Elected representatives of Sinn Fein were not invited to participate in the Forum, on the grounds that they supported violence or, as they saw it, armed struggle against British violence in Northern Ireland. On the other hand, prominent Northern Ireland Protestant politicians who were invited to the Forum refused to attend.

So, side by side with Prior's Northern Ireland Assembly — a powerless talking shop for Northern Protestant politicans — there was a kind of all-Ireland (if Sinn Fein-less) Catholic alternative assembly, the Forum, whose very existence was an indictment of British rule in the North.

Sinn Fein's 1983 electoral success among Irish Catholics in the North was matched by that of Mrs. Thatcher, leader of what was called "the Provisional wing" of the Tory party. Thatcher and the Tories, with only forty-three percent of the popular vote in Britain, won an overwhelming majority in the House of Commons. Thatcher's success practically guaranteed both the failure of the Northern Ireland Assembly and the continued frustration of moderate efforts to end the conflict. Her personality and policies were bound, however, to propel Sinn Fein to continuing and perhaps increasing electoral success. The fifteen unionist politicians who managed, along with John Hume and Gerry Adams, to get elected to the Westminster Parliament in June 1983, could not possibly be a significant voice in a 600-member Parliament completely dominated by Thatcher's Tories.

In Northern Ireland poor Prior was left in the vacuum between his Assembly — as impotent for change as the British rule that sustained it — and the resurgent Provos whose politics represented something entirely new in the Northern Ireland equation. Looming over Prior too, was the New Ireland Forum the Provos' success had inspired.

Prior might have done well at an earlier stage. But he was saddled with the militaristic intransigence of Mrs. Thatcher, and faced with a residue of ill-will left by her and by his predecessors. He inherited a situation where many Protestants, including the leaders of a Protestant paramilitary force, were talking about a future without a British government of any kind.

The loyalist version of a post-conflict Northern Ireland differed of course from the republican version. But a growing number of influential working-class Protestants had become heartily sick of the British Way of Life: sick of being treated, in Rudyard Kipling's phrase, as "lesser breeds without the law."

147

148

(Left) Scene at a crossroads below Newry, Co. Down (near the border with the Irish Republic) where a British Army disposal expert was killed in late May 1981 while trying to defuse an IRA car bomb.

10
The Centre Cannot Hold

AS THE Northern Ireland conflict lurched into its sixteenth year, it was clear that the British were hopelessly without authority to resolve it. They were clearly more of an obstacle to its resolution than either of the domestic antagonists.

After nearly fifty years of irresponsible neglect, in 1969 the British Government had moved in in the role of impartial big brother. Yet Britain soon involved itself in the trouble by weighing in, with its enforcers, on the side of the group whose government and whose enforcers had precipitated the problem in the first place.

The British Government set itself up as mediator in Northern Ireland. But it put the weight of its intervention on the military, who proceeded to introduce heavyweight gunfire and a war mentality. There followed drastic measures, like wholesale internment sweeps, brutal interrogation methods and the sinister technology of political torture. Paratroopers were given police functions and then allowed to murder innocent civilians. The professedly fair-minded British employed juryless trials, perjured police testimony, bought witnesses, criminalization of political suspects and a penal regime to rival Devil's Island. They also employed black propaganda, dirty tricks specialists, and clandestine political assassins. They permitted the SAS, Army and their directly controlled police to summarily shoot IRA and INLA suspects and innocents in cold blood. The British Government's sponsorship of military intervention and military policies had helped bring the Irish Republican Army out of retirement and had in the process given birth — and supplied not only motivation but the matrix and imagery of war — to the Provisional IRA and the INLA, and to the Ulster Defence Association and other armed Protestant forces. The Army's policy of torture created the atmosphere and supplied the sophisticated model for the crude sectarian torture and outright butchery of some Protestant gangs. The British Government's own imports of hopelessness and final impotence communicated itself to all the participants and sufferers as a prevailing sense of despair.

Yet the British professed to be a civilised and decent people. And with reason. Only occasionally did they massacre or assassinate their enemies in Northern Ireland. It was not regular policy. And they finally rejected (after years of indulging it) the policy of interrogatory torture. British practice in Ireland could respond, in the intermediate or long run at least, to the demands of the decent opinion of mankind.

Furthermore, because of Britain's record of restraint in dealing with the civilian population, the British Government and Army could not be called Hitlerian or Stalinist. The British military and police forces showed far more restraint towards civilians and even towards antagonists in Northern Ireland than the United States had shown in Vietnam.

The policy applied by the British Government in Northern Ireland was far better British policy, in fact, than had been applied in places like Palestine or India or Malaysia. Far better than the vindictive British policy of saturation bombing of German cities under Arthur "Bomber" Harris in World War II — though the distinction might have been lost on Catholic young men in Northern Ireland prisons caught up in the British "security forces" dragnet.

In any case, it was not necessary to accuse the British of ill will to see what had been wrong. Since the breakup of their empire — and even to some extent before — they had been preventing what the UDA called "proper politics" being given a chance in Northern Ireland. So that even many Protestants had become weary of violence and tired of a British rule that sustained the violence in being, while keeping them, as well as Catholics, in subservience to a faraway government in London. For them now, as had been the case for Catholics for sixty years and more, *there was no consent of the governed*. This was not democracy but despotism. And Direct Rule from London meant that it was an alien despotism. Margaret Thatcher, in her authoritarian self-righteousness and in her quintessentially English middle-class matron persona, magnificently epitomized both the alienness and the despotism: hard cake with the bitter tea, and bad child's nasty nurse shouting "Eat it!"

She was a brutal enough nurse. The death toll Thatcher took of her own and enemy troops in the Falklands in 1982 rivalled in a few weeks the entire fifteen-year death toll in Northern Ireland: In the Falklands some twenty-three hundred dead, including over two hundred fifty British troops — not counting the hideously maimed and burned. She did this to prop up her tottering regime at home, a regime of unemployment, industrial devastation and a faltering pound sterling. In early 1983 a cartoon in the English satirical magazine *Private Eye* showed a head of Thatcher atop a cemetery monument with the inscription

(Above) Mahood cartoon published in the London *Daily Mail* two days after the dramatic breakout by 38 Republican prisoners from the Maze Prison at Long Kesh on Sunday 25 September 1983. The Maze had been considered one of Europe's most secure prisons, and it was the biggest breakout in Britain's penal history. Nineteen of the escapees eluded an intensive manhunt mounted afterward by the highly embarrassed British authorities. The British tabloids, along with some Unionist politicians, were apoplectic about the escape, but a great many Protestants and virtually all Catholics in the North reacted with a certain glee. The prisoners used a blue prison food truck for the escape, and Belfast walls blossomed with graffiti, one of which proclaimed in white paint: "Open Up the Long Kesh Gate: Meals on Wheels for 38."

Everyone who is not an idiot will admit, to begin with, that no government can be strong, or indeed govern at all, without the consent and co-operation of the governed. . . . Laws are enforced, not by the police, but by the citizens who call the police when the law is broken. If the citizens connive at breaches of the law and shield the lawbreaker instead of denouncing him, it is all up with the Government.

The executive may refuse to admit checkmate for a time. If it has sufficient manpower at its disposal it can bring about a state of things in which out of every five persons in the country one is a spy, one a policeman, and two are soldiers.

If [the government] has sufficient money it can put the whole population in prison and support them there. But that is not governing: it is mere coercion, destructive to production, incompatible with prosperity, ruinous alike to the coercer and the coerced. It cannot settle the country, develop the country, secure property and person in the country, satisfy the country, or in short, achieve any of the ends of government.

This is so obvious that the advocacy of such coercion by sane men will be taken as evidence of a design to ruin the country, and a very stupid one when the circumstances are such as to make it impossible for even a Cromwell to go through with the process . . .

George Bernard Shaw
1919

below: "They died that she might save face."

In Northern Ireland Protestants as well as Catholics could see what was going on. More and more factories were closed, and clearly Thatcher was suffering no pangs about the rising percentages of Protestant loyalists now on the dole queues. The violence establishment entrenched itself, the uniformed forces especially. The remote control managers were as indifferent and inept as ever.

In this situation a great many Protestants were quite willing to swallow the United Ireland solution if that's what it came down to. Others, rejecting a united Ireland, nevertheless wanted to find a way to make their own political arrangements with their Catholic compatriots.

In a partly plaintive, partly sarcastic editorial written toward the end of the first decade of the conflict, a *Fortnight* magazine writer asked whether it was right for the British to continue to deny the people of Northern Ireland "the indulgence of a democratic framework" and went on to say:

The only way to operate a democratic framework is by doing it. We have never had democratic institutions in Northern Ireland. All we have had have been institutions incorporating the dictatorship of a majority. We must be allowed to evolve institutions which are truly democratic in that they do not entail supremacy by one group over another whether that group be ethnic, economic or social . . .

> *Turning and turning in the widening gyre*
> *The falcon cannot hear the falconer;*
> *Things fall apart, the centre cannot hold;*
> *Mere anarchy is loosed upon the world,*
> *The blood-dimmed tide is loosed, and everywhere*
> *The ceremony of innocence is drowned . . .*
> *William Butler Yeats*

But the British mentality was very different from that of the Northern Irish, particularly the "native" Irish, who sometimes appeared to Britons to take on almost oriental characteristics. There were vast differences of outlook.

And there were great problems stemming from matters of detail. For example, the British electoral timetable was completely out of tune with Irish rhythms. There were sometimes devastating consequences, as in the changes in government that brought shifts from a cautious and careful to an aggressive "get tough" British policy in 1970, from a decisive and committed to a weak and vacillating government in 1974.

The British liked to suggest, when it suited them, that Northern Ireland was really no different from Britain; British propagandists and the British media often seemed reluctant to let go of the idea that Ireland as a whole was a British isle.

But there was nothing more than a patina or gloss of Britishness even about Northern Ireland. Just how shallow a gloss was shown most sharply by political differences, which sometimes produced opposite outcomes from the same political events.

In 1981, Thatcher's posture of triumphal contempt towards the dying Irish hunger strikers won her a measure of admiration in Britain but shocked reasonable people in Northern Ireland and antagonized many Southern Irish Catholics; her bloody-mindedness towards the hunger strikers in fact helped bring down two successive governments — cooperative, pro-Thatcher governments — in the Republic.

The bitter seed their interventions sowed in Ireland had a curious effect on the British. Surveying the damage they themselves had done, British governments blamed the Irish. The British tended to argue circularly about these interventions. Northern Ireland was their problem, the British would say, and only they could solve it: Only they could mediate between the native tribes. Then when they found themselves hopelessly unable to resolve the problem — when they found themselves instead exacerbating it — they blamed their failure on the intractability of the Irish. The problem, they would now say, was that the natives refused to cooperate with Britain.

If any conflict is to be resolved, there must be a centre that can bring the wheeling destructive energies under control: a mobilizing, harmonising centre around which, or whom, efforts for a resolution can rally. The evidence by now was massive: Britain could never be such a holding centre in Northern Ireland.

Liam de Paor had written in 1972:

> Planters and natives can undoubtedly come to an agreement in Ireland, perhaps an agreement to continue in some form the partition of the country, but it seems essential that those who are responsible for government in Ireland should be rooted in the country and committed to it — and ultimately dependent on Irish resources and initiatives to solve Ireland's problems.
>
> What keeps the sterile quarrel of Orange and Green alive is the constant presence of the third party, Great Britain.

(Left) Aerial view of one of the H-blocks at the Maze prison at Long Kesh in 1981.

IRA man at scene of devastation. Belfast, 1972.

Toward a Solution

What are the roots that clutch,
What branches grow
Out of this stony rubbish?
T.S. Eliot

(Left) UDA march in Belfast in 1972.

11
Toward a New Politics

IN THE 1980s the British Government could no longer maintain the fantasy that it was a neutral big brother in Northern Ireland. It is the principal antagonist. Its destructive power — coupled with its impotence in Irish affairs and its incompetence in solving the problem — has lengthened the conflict to a decade and a half.

The people of Northern Ireland, and Ireland generally, are faced with the fact that the supposed centre will have to be displaced.

But where can a holding or rallying centre be found?

An observer from some other part of the planet might think that the natural centre should lie with the Irish government of the twenty-six county Republic.

But is the Irish government up to the task?

Ireland is unavoidably a neighbour to a Britain eleven times its size in population. So it is especially difficult for most Irish people — north or south or east or west of the six-county border — to think clearly about post-conflict relationships in a context of normality. The abnormal — a repressive Stormont regime followed by the British regime of violence — has been presented by Britain as normal for over sixty years. And the British view of normalcy provides the media backdrop against which Irish judgments are made.

This media factor makes it extremely difficult for people living on the island of Ireland to think their own thoughts. Their eyes and ears are daily assailed by a Briticized view of themselves. Television and radio broadcasts in most of Ireland are dominated by the BBC

157

and ITV, i.e., by British-centred networks. The local six-county Northern Ireland commercial television license is issued by and subject to review by a British authority. This situation is further complicated by the bizarre Irish law that prohibits elected members of a Republic political organization like Sinn Fein, which has relatively free access to the British airwaves, to utter a single syllable on RTE, the Irish TV and radio station. Most Irish patriotic songs are also banned. Although no Republican may be heard from, virtually any rabid anti-nationalist can have his say.

In addition, political commentators on RTE and their backup staffs tend to bring a certain pro-British bias to their work. They are usually liberals, and in Ireland liberalism is defined in terms both of middle class consumer values and of the pervasive British notions of what constitutes legitimacy, acceptable police behaviour, terrorism, and so forth.

Irish political behaviour, like Irish media commentary, has come to be characterized by an extraordinary effort to treat the lunatic abnormality of the British regime in the North as though it were quite normal. The British-leaning liberal idealism of some politicians in the Republic has made them so pro-British when in power as to be imitatively fascist in practice, as in the ruthless murdering of anti-treaty prisoners by the first Cosgrave government during the Civil War in 1922-23, and as in the 1973-77 coalition government's use of "heavy gang" police tactics: beating Irish paramilitary suspects as brutally as did Mason's and Newman's RUC. At critical times during the sixty-odd years of Stormont and British rule, twenty-six county Irish governments have often performed disgracefully: in their acceptance of the outrageous decision by the Boundary Commission in 1925; in their allowing the victimization of Catholics in 1969; in their feeble performance against Thatcher during the hunger strike of 1981. At such times their indecent regard for British opinion was matched by an astonishing disregard for Northern Irish sons and daughters.

Given Irish politicians' often ludicrously accommodating behaviour towards the British — and towards unionist intransigence — and given also the horror the Irish people of the twenty-six counties understandably have of being embroiled in this bloody conflict, it might seem absurd to count among the concerned parties those three and a half million Irish people who occupy three quarters of the island of Ireland. But these are local people, fellow islanders paying some quarter of a billion Irish pounds a year to maintain a border they don't constitutionally recognize; their economy suffers, crime related to the North increases, and Northern violence spills continually into their awareness, a regular and depressing reminder of their failure to do anything to remedy the rank injustice of the situation there.

And the Republic in fact lays constitutional claim to the six counties of Northern Ireland — a claim successive governments of the Republic have reiterated. (They also keep saying

(Left) Charles J. Haughey, leader of Fianna Fail Party in the Republic of Ireland and Irish Taoiseach from December 1979 to June 1981 and again from March to December 1982.

(Left) Dr. Garret Fitzgerald, leader of Fine Gael Party in the Republic of Ireland and Irish Taoiseach from June 1981 to February 1982 and again from December 1982 on.

> *The situation is urgent because time is running out. We must face the reality that Northern Ireland, a political entity, has failed, and that a new beginning is needed. The time has surely come for the sovereign governments to work together to find a formula and lift the situation onto a new plane that will bring permanent peace and stability to the people of these islands.*
>
> *Charles J. Haughey*

that they have no intention of attempting to unify Ireland by force.)

Irish governments are open to the accusation that as far as the North is concerned they rule a brass monkey Republic, with hands over eyes, ears and mouth: "See no evil, hear no evil, speak no evil." Most people in Dublin seem to want not to know. But in the twenty-six county Irish Republic as a whole, there is a majority who — though they may lack immediate power to do anything about it — cannot stomach the situation in the northeast of the island. They retain a race memory of an all-Ireland cultural union and have a guilty awareness of having deserted their own nationalist people in the North. They have another race memory — no less vivid for being primitive and unconscious — of rape or gross violation: of genocide, plunder, famine, subjugation and terrible poverty during the centuries of British control of the island.

These factors, working in the Irish psyche, dispose most people in the twenty-six county Republic to want the island rid of British rule. Even the consumer slumbers of comfortable Dubliners are troubled by the persistent nightmare of Northern Ireland. Deep down they know that, until the problem is genuinely resolved, any dream of a tranquil, prosperous Ireland, or of real peace between the English and the Irish people, will be illusory. And the Irish know in their hearts that it is not the IRA and not the planter people — who, after all, have lived on the island for centuries — who are ultimately responsible for the stalemate.

During the past sixty-odd years, British commercial, landowning and military interests have manipulated the North, as they manipulated the whole of Ireland for centuries — for their own aggrandizement. While most Irish in the South condemn the violence and atrocities of the armed nationalist rebels in the North, they understand, as the British do not, why there *is* armed rebellion up there. Despite the heavy British line in the media — despite ineffectual Irish Government policy and forelock-tugging diplomacy — there is in the South a deep and abiding resentment of the insolence of the British for remaining in Ireland and a longing for deliverance of the rest of the island from their grasp.

The British, however incompetent and unwelcome, remain a reality in Northern Ireland. Their government, their methods and their military wing are all palpably part of the scene. Even Provo politicians deal with the Northern Ireland Office and British institutions as de facto reality.

The British seem bloodily intent (as in the Falklands) on maintaining their proprietary claim. It is not unlike the United States' claim on Panama: "We stole it fair and square, so it's ours." The Americans have since conceded Panama to the Panamanians. But in Ireland the British still hold territory they took by force. Why? The reason for this cannot be economic. Especially since Thatcher launched her scorched-earth industrial policy, Britain's economic interests in Northern Ireland are more and more residual. And Northern Ireland is losing Britain some two billion pounds a year.

Is the real reason military?

British strategists, and the Americans who do most of their thinking for them, are intermittently assailed by fears that a wholly independent and neutral Ireland would endanger their Western approaches. The American military, with its omnivorous appetite for territorial advantage, finds it difficult to conceive that the Irish might like to stand aside from the global competition between the two superpowers.

The Western military sees the island of Ireland as surrounded by submarine lanes in which the undersea dreadnoughts of NATO are forever jockeying for position with submarines belonging to an insatiably self-aggrandizing Russia. Above ground, the US and British military see Ireland as handy terrain on which to site batteries of nuclear rockets or, failing that, as an island cobwebbed with radar to give earlier warning of Russian Backfire bombers.

Irish military analysts find plenty of evidence these days that the Irish in the South, who can't do much about subs they can neither control nor see, are already offering Ireland not as a nuclear but as a communications base. If they want to sell their neutrality, the Irish, simply by insisting, could have the North plus tens of billions of dollars. Instead, dancing on the edge of NATO, Irish governments maintain their amateur status, allowing in very dangerous radar installations: turning the trick almost for free. If the politicians are going to sell the Republic, they ought at least to go professional.

It's a sad situation because the Irish don't really have to barter away their neutrality. Legitimate British and American military needs can be met by alternative strategies. And, once the problem of the North is settled, the people of Ireland will have various other ways to get the financing they'll need to rebuild the devastated North and repair the damage done the rest of the island by the conflict.

British governments, themselves gone cuckoo with enthusiasm for first-strike missiles and the whole nightmare apparatus of the mushroom holocaust, regularly lecture the Irish on safety and security — like arsonists teaching children about the dangers of matches.

They like to argue that if they withdrew their army and guns and war machines from Northern Ireland, the place would soon be awash in blood. Due to the outreach of the British propaganda network, the bloodbath theory has become settled conviction among many.

Yet statistically the theory works the other way. Before the British brought their army into play in late 1969, the

(Right) **The body of a seven-month old baby is carried away after an IRA bomb exploded at a Shankill Road furniture factory, killing three others and injuring twenty-two in December 1971.**

conflict had produced six or seven deaths. Since the advent of the British Army as pacifying power, some *twenty-three hundred* have died, and more than twenty-five thousand have been tortured, maimed, mutilated, burned, blinded, brain-damaged. The British brought the sword of war: modern, technologically sophisticated war. It was after their coming that murder and devastation became the order of the day.

Given the institutionalized violence of the present regime, some in Ireland argue that it is time to get the British out, then take the short, sharp shock of civil war. As a German proverb puts it: Better an end in terror than terror without end. So once the British are out, there can be a quick civil war — a bloodletting, not a bloodbath — ending the violence once and for all. That's how some people argue. But why should any increase in violence follow the withdrawal of the most violent participant?

In any case the burden of proof is on British apologists to show how a phased withdrawal, coupled with a return of democratic control to the domestic parties, could conceivably lead to a bloodbath.

British apologists work on a number of very dubious assumptions. They assume for example, that Ian Paisley's phantom legions represent hard reality. Their dismal scenarios assume that in the aftermath of a British departure everything

would go ludicrously wrong, and that the Protestant and Catholic Irish would abandon not only their good sense but all vestiges of fear and even of apathy — their well-established, western, television-conditioned consumerist apathy — and would mindlessly take to the streets like crazed savages on a murderous warpath.

Northern Irish Protestants, who according to Britain and its apologists were to supply the shock-troops for this *Götterdämmerung,* have been accused of many things, but never of being inept at arithmetic. They are as practical a people as any on earth.

Supposing the worst case for Protestants — a sudden, overnight abandonment by Britain and a peremptory withdrawal of all uniformed forces — the bloodbath scenarios assume that Protestants would abandon all calculation and, on an island where they represent about a fifth of the population, would embark on a bloody adventure which, by awakening the slumbering nationalism of southern Catholics, might lead directly to a slaughter of the northern Protestant people.

Few Protestants have any taste for bloodshed; they are as sick of it as Catholics north and south. Any estimate of potentially violent Protestants in Northern Ireland must put them in a tiny minority. Ian Paisley's rhetoric of violence would hardly be enough to drive the relative handful of violent-minded Protestants to the point where they would forget to count the odds in a contest of such proportions. The Northern Irish, Protestants and Catholics, are surely cunning enough in any case to prevent such a worst-case situation from arising, partly by seeing to it that the British departure is properly phased. Even the Provisional IRA, when last heard from on the subject, envisioned a time span of two-and-a-half years for British withdrawal.

Though the removal of the British from the scene is absolutely crucial to solving the problem, they will have to have some voice in the terms of their disengagement — not least between the domestic parties would need, or at least would probably welcome, an idemnity (or contribution) from Britain — on the order of, say, ten billion pounds over a five year period — to help them dig themselves out of the morass. The net loss to Britain is running up to that level now — two billion pounds a year — without any foreseeable end to the drain of funds. They would save enormous sums in the long run by making a similar but closed-end contribution to a new peaceful political order set up and managed by the Irish parties themselves alone.

Such a level of funding, especially when taken together with substantial financial help from other sources like the EEC and the United States, would benefit Britain enormously. The British would leave behind them, after the centuries of violence towards Ireland, a residue of goodwill. But the Irish or Northern

(Below)   RUC man in Derry firing plastic bullet during street violence in April 1981.

(Right) Member of Provisional IRA exhibiting submachine gun during a kind of military fashion show at Casement Park, Belfast, at end of Provisional parade on 12 August 1979.

Irish could go it alone if necessary, to protect their neutrality and to avoid any involvement in the absurd and potentially catastrophic East/West nuclear confrontation. The coming of final peace could unleash vast energies North and South, and open brilliant new economic horizons for all the Irish people.

Which of the various organized parties in the North are essential to a solution of the problem?

What might be laid down as one principle is that, whatever use Northern Irish parliamentarians might be in ending a war, the armed antagonists who wage the war have to be deeply involved if the conflict is going to be resolved.

Years ago there was a little publicized but significant attempt on the part of two of the domestic antagonists to end the conflict. It involved both the Provisional IRA and the ULCCC—the Ulster Loyalist Central Coordinating Committee.

These negotiations had their antecedents as far back as 1972 when a group led by the then shadow Prime Minister Harold Wilson met with a group led by Daithi O Connaill of Provisional Sinn Fein.

Attempts at talks continued spasmodically; there were the negotiations between the British and the Provisionals at Chelsea in early July 1972, and further meetings between the Provos and Harold Wilson later than month.

In January 1975 arrangements were made for the appointment of a tripartite commission representing the various antagonists involved in the conflict. This commission was to look for common ground and make recommendations for resolving the problem. The membership of the commission was to consist of Seán MacBride, a Dublin barrister, who had won the Nobel Peace prize the previous year; Desmond Boal, a Belfast barrister regarded as the best defense lawyer in the six counties of Northern Ireland; and Jo Grimond, a former leader of the British Liberal Party.

While the commission was never formally set up, partly due to some question of Grimond's appropriateness as the British member, partly due to other factors, shadowy contacts had now been made between the Provisional IRA and the Protestant ULCCC. The ULCCC claimed to represent—though it didn't really represent—the UDA. Nevertheless in the mid-seventies these Protestant-Catholic contacts were given new impetus by the UDA's publication of its NUPRG program for an independent Ulster.

In the discussions there seemed to be agreement on two major points. First, both the Provisionals and the ULCCC loyalist group were agreed on the withdrawal of all British troops from Northern Ireland. Second, they were agreed on the release of all political prisoners held in the six counties.

Their principal disagreement was about what would replace the British government as ruling authority in Northern Ireland. The Provisional IRA of the time wanted a nine-county Ulster provincial parliament linked to some extent with the Dublin Irish government. The loyalist group thought in terms of an independent six-county state linked to neither London nor Dublin.

In late 1976 the Provisionals and the ULCCC invited Seán MacBride and Desmond Boal to make themselves available to assist the parties in finding a solution. The two groups didn't want a British representative in on any discussions until a later stage. Only when agreement was reached would the British Government be involved in the negotiating process.

The two groups gave MacBride and Boal only a restricted brief: They were merely to advise the two parties. MacBride and Boal accepted the assignment on the strict understanding that they were both equally acceptable to the two parties; their mutual acceptability was confirmed. The two negotiators met on several occasions—in Antrim, in Dublin, and in Paris where Mr. MacBride was working as chairman of an inter-

(Above) Desmond Boal.

(Above) Seán MacBride.

national UNESCO committee on communications problems. Among the ideas MacBride put forward was that the European Convention on Human Rights — an international instrument for which he had been largely responsible — could form the basis for a federal relationship between Dublin and a six or nine county "Ulster," because the Human Rights Convention had been accepted by London, Dublin and Belfast governments, and because it embodied all the safeguards essential to the protection of minorities in Ireland North and South.

MacBride suggested that, if necessary, additional powers could be given to the European Commission on Human Rights and the European Court of Human Rights to resolve any issues that might arise. The basic mechanisms were already in existence in the Council of Europe. Discussion between Boal and MacBride revolved around links that might be established between the six or nine county unit and the Republic of Ireland. As the Sunday *Times* put it (25 July 1978):

> The lines of long term solution were emerging; a North which would be independent, and at the same time loosely federated with the South. It was around these two infinitely variable concepts — independence and federation — that the debate was increasingly to revolve.

MacBride and Boal felt that it was essential to establish a total ceasefire in order to enable negotiations to proceed. They were able to agree on a statement committing both sides to such a ceasefire, leaving open only the date. Several factors prevented agreement from proceeding further at this stage. First of all there were differences of opinion among various elements in the Provisional IRA and Provisional Sinn Fein. Second, there was the new loyalist strike of May 1977, organized by Ian Paisley, which created divisions within the Protestant community and distracted the attention of the ULCCC from the negotiations. Third, both the British Government and the arch-conservative Irish Government then in power had been bypassed; so neither of them were enthusiastic about the negotiations taking place. Ironically enough, the then Irish Government particularly resented the fact that the Provisionals were conducting negotiations on their own with the loyalist committee.

The negotiators themselves felt that the political leadership in Britain would probably have welcomed a settlement which would end the violence in the North, though MacBride at least doubted the enthusiasm of the British Secret Service for the ending of a regime of violence in whose continuance they had a heavy financial investment. Other sectors of the British establishment, too, were dead set against the British losing control of Northern Ireland.

The 1976-77 negotiations were in MacBride's view very much on the right track: "To try to get a settlement without the hard men," he said, "was the same as trying to get a settlement in the Middle East without the PLO being involved, or in Namibia without SWAPO being involved." The aim, MacBride said, had to be first to win agreement between the two extreme factions on the ground. When this was achieved, then the British and Irish governments could become involved.

> *[There is a] squalid pretence that the problems of Ulster flow from the flaring up of mysterious sectarian differences and not from the misery, anger and frustration produced by the sorry mess of fifty years of British rule, the white-washing of the massacre of Bloody Sunday of January 1972, the arbitrariness and brutality concomitant with internment without trial, the hypocritical shunning of the Strasbourg report of 1976 which found Britain guilty of the crime of torture and inhuman treatment in Northern Ireland, the method used to extract "confessions" for the political Diplock trials, the killing of civilians by rubber and plastic bullets and speeding ferretcars: [Such factors are] equally if not more responsible for the deaths of the hunger-strikers and all the violence and misery that followed.*
>
> *So long as those beams in the English eye remain, so long does the English condemnation of hunger-strikers lack moral credibility . . .*
>
> *The New Blackfriars*
> *London 1981*

> *The English are a remarkable race; but they have no common sense. We [Irish] never lose our common sense. The English people say . . . we [would] cut each other's throats. Who has a better right to cut them? They are very glad to get us to cut the throats of their enemies. Why should we not have the same privilege among ourselves? What will prevent it? The natural resistance of the other Irishmen.*
>
> *George Bernard Shaw*
> *1912*

Negotiations among the men of violence, of the paramilitary forces especially, are crucial if the violence in Northern Ireland is to be ended. Given the removal of the British from the scene, the problem in Northern Ireland would be greatly simplified; it would be relatively easy, and also necessary, for the local gunmen to negotiate with one another.

What special difficulties arise from the idea of having paramilitaries at the conference table?

First of all there is the question of their willingness to bargain and negotiate.

The UDA appears to be willing enough to move toward politics. The IRA sat down with Whitelaw in 1972, with Protestant clergymen in 1974 and with Rees's people in 1975. There have been other instances of IRA negotiation. Its leaders have often said that what they want is an all-Ireland conference coupled with a specific promise of British withdrawal by a definite date.

(Left)   Early on in the conflict, British soldiers stand ready to use CS gas pistols against Protestants in the Shankill Road: Belfast, September 1970.

Some extreme voices in the IRA and INLA are heard from time to time talking about destroying all Irish government North and South, but these voices are taken seriously only by a few lightheaded politicians (some, naturally enough, in high places in Dublin and London). The idea of a Provisional war to the death against all authority on the island is promoted chiefly by British and other theorists of intractability, who welcome any hint that seems to bolster their thesis that the conflict is insoluble.

When Danny Morrison, publicity officer for Provisional Sinn Fein, said at Sinn Fein's Ard Fheis or annual conference in 1982 that there was no reason why the Provos could not go forward to take power in Ireland with an Armalite in one hand and a ballot paper in the other, he got a lot of attention. Was he implying that the Provos wanted to replace an armed British fascism with an armed Republican fascism? Morrison in fact was addressing himself to those in Sinn Fein and the IRA who wanted to keep the Provos out of politics. He was trying to justify political action as an addition to the traditional physical force strategy. At the November 1983 Ard Fheis Gerry Adams, President of Sinn Fein, said:

> Armed struggle is a necessary and morally correct form of resistance in the six counties . . . [but] Republicans are not interested in an armed struggle in a twenty-six county context aimed at the takeover of the state . . . We, as Republicans, have a decided preference that [an independent Ireland] should be a democratic socialist Republic . . . But we accept that in a post-British withdrawal situation, with Irish democracy restored, we will be bound by the democratic wishes of the Irish people.

Republicans who'd borne the brunt of the protest in the prison—IRA and INLA men who'd been on the blanket in Long Kesh—seemed to share this view. While locked up in the H-blocks, these protesting prisoners had taken great abuse from the warders. The prisoners held nightly discussions and debates, the purpose being to understand who they were, what they were doing, why they were suffering, and what they wanted out of the conflict. They concluded that they could support no system which permitted the brutalization or exploitation of one person by another. They would continue to use force to get the British out of Ireland, attacking anyone using force to maintain British control. Then they'd turn to persuasion. The idea of using armed force afterward to impose a certain kind of post-conflict regime in Ireland was against everything they had taught themselves in the hard school of the prison cells.

Can it be left to the men of violence to deal with their own imperialists in the aftermath of the conflict?

There is a second major problem that especially concerns the nationalist paramilitaries.

(Above) Image of fear: Some wives of RUC and part-time UDR men in heavily Catholic areas near six-county border felt they had to guard their husbands against sudden IRA and INLA attacks.

In the late 70s and early 80s there was a campaign against local members of the UDR and RUC in predominantly Catholic regions along the twenty-six county border — a campaign directed by the Provos and INLA. Several dozen men were killed. These men were Protestants; so Protestants, reasonably enough, saw the killings as sectarian. Protestants recalled mass murders like Bloody Friday and, in their view specifically anti-Protestant atrocities like La Mon (an accident, but an atrocity; and La Mon was a centre for Protestants around Comber). Then there was the killing in late 1981 of the Rev. Robert Bradford, M.P., a personal ally of Ian Paisley and a rhetorician of violence but, to Protestants, one of their own. So that Protestants, who for more than fifty years sustained a Unionist Party government that oppressed

> *To the British Government and to the majority of the British people the problem is a simple one of armed subversion. They take the classic view that no democratically elected government can submit to violence or the threat of violence and survive; that negotiation with armed terrorists is out of the question; and that therefore violence must end before any attempt is made to redress the grievances of the insurgents. In the familiar idiom of operations in aid of the civil power, it is for the security forces to restore the rule of law and create a stable situation in which the normal political processes can be resumed . . .*
>
> *Alun Chalfont*
> *1972*

> *It is of course fatuous to say that violence and terrorism are always ineffective, that you cannot "bomb your way to the conference table." One has only to think of the position today of that notable and entirely ruthless terrorist, Menachêm Begin.*
>
> *Claud Cockburn*
> *1981*

Northern Irish Catholics, have in recent years come to think of themselves as the oppressed. Ian Paisley put it this way in a meeting with Margaret Thatcher in 1981:

> The last time I met you in this very room I told you that I represented the most wronged, the most maligned, the most tried and the most betrayed people in all the United Kingdom — namely the Ulster Protestants. They have given voluntarily their sons and daughters to the RUC, their young manhood to the Army and UDR.
>
> They have been bombed and burned, murdered and mutilated and yet it seems to them that no British Government of recent years either appreciates their position or would really stand up and support their rights and liberties under the Constitution.

Given the Protestant feeling that Provisional and INLA actions were directed against Protestants, how could Protestants even accept the idea of negotiations with them?

The answer is the same as for any people after any war: The combatants have to negotiate with one another. It could be added that Protestants in Northern Ireland do not enjoy the luxury of being able, from the distant comfort of Whitehall or an English manor house, to indulge a principle of not talking to gunmen. The hard humour of many Ulster Protestants is in fact such that they'd just as soon talk to the gunmen as to John Hume. Some Protestants

(Right) Gerry Adams, MP for West Belfast

in the North have personally known Provos, like the Protestant security chief who once worked with Gerry Adams — now a Provisional Sinn Fein Member of Parliament and the foremost Republican spokesman: a man who said that he would trust Adams to keep his word.

It is the Catholic gunmen who, most Protestants insist, are causing all the trouble. Without a Cromwellian massacre of Catholics generally, they can't be brought down. So, like UDA and the UVF, they will have to be talked to: the IRA. And even the INLA.

> *It is very hard for the British (I use the word generically, for all those who feel their prime loyalty to be to London, the Queen, and all that) — it is very hard for a people at once insular and imperial to realize that within the very perimeters of their own small islands there are people fundamentally different than they in aspiration, in culture, and in race. For a thousand years they have considered the Irishman only a sort of deluded Briton, and their attitude toward the Welsh, who are not even separated from them by a strip of water, is just as obfuscatory . . .*
>
> *It is this very lack of sensitivity, I think, the exact failing which so often vitiated the achievements of the British world empire, that makes the British the very last people qualified to solve the Irish problem.*
>
> *It was the British themselves who created that problem, in all its complications, and it is really their own wishful self-delusion, powerfully supported of course by the fears and passions of their clients the Ulster Protestants, which leads them to think of Northern Ireland even now as genuinely a part of Britain — a part of England, I sometimes feel they would really like to say . . .*
>
> *Jan Morris*

> *In Ireland over the centuries, we have tried every possible formula: direct rule, indirect rule, genocide, apartheid, puppet parliaments, real parliaments, martial law, civil law, colonization, land reform, partition. Nothing has worked. The only solution we have not tried is absolute and unconditional withdrawal . . .*
>
> Paul Johnson
> The Spectator

When the British go, their guarantee to the Protestant unionists in Northern Ireland will go with them. Catholics have always seen the guarantee as an obstacle to rational politics. Here, for example is John Hume's view:

> The basis of British policy is concealed under layers of good intentions, ingenious initiatives, commissions of inquiry, attempted reforms, financial aid and a good deal of genial bewilderment. I do not use the word "concealed" maliciously. Many sincere and concerned British politicians and observers have the impression that they have tried everything possible to get the Irish to agree together: that is a measure of the extent to which the basic assumption of their policy has become imperceptible to the British themselves.
>
> The ground of their policy is the reiterated guarantee that Northern Ireland shall remain a part of the United Kingdom so long as a majority of the electorate of Northern Ireland so desire. That would seem, at first reading, to be an eminently democratic and responsible undertaking. The fact is, however, that it has not worked. It has not produced peace or stable government in Northern Ireland. Moreover, it has provided the basis for a half century of injustice, discrimination and repressive law, a situation in which [the Catholic community] have been the persistent losers and victims . . .
>
> While this guarantee exists, there is no incentive for Unionists to enter into genuine dialogue with those with whom they share the island of Ireland. The suffering and frustration of the people of Northern Ireland overwhelmingly attest to the fact that the guarantee was, to put it very bluntly, a tragic mistake. The price has been paid too long, and in too many lives . . .

The guarantee does have the great attraction of making the British appear to stand foursquare on democratic principle. Yet the gerrymander that created Northern Ireland in the first place included very extensive Catholic majority areas, taken in *without the consent* of the Catholics there.

The loss of the guarantee might, paradoxically, prove to be exactly what is needed to guarantee Protestants the security they are still vainly seeking in the 1980s. Obviously the prospect of the loss of the guarantee as such did not trouble Andy Tyrie & Company, when they developed the NUPRG document that outlined their proposal for an independent Ulster.

(Left) John Hume, MP for Foyle , pictured in 1978 when he was beginning his successful run for the European Parliament. In 1983 Hume successfully advocated a formal EEC investigation into the economic and political crisis in Northern Ireland.

173

> *No British Government ought ever to forget that this perilous moment, like many before it, is the outworking of a history for which our country is primarily responsible. England seized Ireland for its own military benefit; it planted Protestant settlers there to make it strategically secure; it humiliated and penalized the native Irish and their Catholic religion. And then, when it could no longer hold on to the whole island, kept back part to be a home for the settlers' descendants, a non-viable solution from which the Protestants have suffered as much as anyone.*
>
> *John Austin Baker*
> *Chaplain to the Speaker,*
> *British House of Commons,*
> *during 1980 hunger strike*

In any case there can be no resolving the Northern Ireland conflict while the British guarantors persist in administering a regime marked by violence to which they are the principal contributor.

As the *Sunday Times* put it in August 1981: "British policy in Northern Ireland — to try to keep it in the United Kingdom by general consent — has not worked, is not working and will not work."

Liam de Paor had put it more pointedly nine years earlier:

> All lines of argument about the Northern Ireland situation in fact lead back to the central question of the use of force and violence.
>
> The process begun by Protestant Ulster in 1911, the process of disregard for established institutions and resort to force, is still working itself out, and must continue inevitably to work itself out in violence and turmoil until the way is opened to negotiation.
>
> This will involve a recognition on the one hand that the Dublin government has a legitimate interest in Northern Ireland, and on the other hand that the nine hundred thousand or so of Ulster's population who reject Dublin are entitled to a special political provision.
>
> A British solution, imposed by British guns, has failed, is failing and will continue to fail.

(Right) A young RUC constable chokes back tears as he stands to attention beside coffin of a colleague killed by a booby trap bomb in September 1981.

> *The Northern Irish are a peculiarly gifted people ... It is ... tragic that they should be doomed by Britain's inattentive presence to go on wasting their time and energies addressing the wrong problems.*
> The Sunday Times

(Left) Rope bridge at Carrick-a-Rede, Co. Antrim, pictured in 1979.

12
Shaping a New Politics

IF THE political regime in Northern Ireland is a regime of violence resulting from and still based on a power conflict among three major factions — with the British as the alien, unnatural and most violent antagonist — then the withdrawal of the British is likely to reduce the problem from exponential to arithmetical proportions. Given the removal of the British faction, movement toward a political solution would involve the shaping of a plan for a new politics on which the local antagonists could agree.

There is no prophet who can confidently predict what parts of the suggestions on offer would work.

For the record, the more viable scenarios include the following:

(a) an independent six, seven or nine county Northern Ireland state
(b) an Irish dimension option, under which all Northern Irish people are free to choose either Irish or British citizenship
(c) an Irish two-parliament confederation
(d) a united Ireland

177

Of the above, a united Ireland might or might not require the use of considerable force. An independent Northern Ireland might, under certain conditions, satisfy Northern Irish Republicans fed up with the South. There is something to be said for and against all these scenarios.

The "Irish dimension option" is interesting, especially since its proponents are Northern Irish Catholics.

They feel that two facts have to be kept in mind:

(1) The reason Northern Irish Catholics have always kept rebelling against British rule is that they see themselves as Irish. They want to be free to be Irish, in Ireland. So the general point of view of those representing the approximately 650,000 Catholics is that British rule has to be removed from Northern Ireland.

(2) Northern Protestants want to remain British and for a hundred years have been acting to ensure that they will remain British. So the general point of view of those representing this group of some 850,000 Protestants is that they have to be allowed to be British and to have their rights as Britons guaranteed.

Obviously, advocates of this option argue, a just solution has to accommodate the points of view of both Catholics and Protestants in Northern Ireland. The right of Catholics to be Irish, and the right of Protestants to be British, have to be guaranteed institutionally and constitutionally. The British regime, with its coercive and repressive features, must be removed from Northern Ireland; but Irish rule cannot be imposed on Northern Protestants.

Therefore British rule and military force must be utterly removed from Ireland, and all repressive laws and enactments — special powers acts, emergency powers acts, law enforcement acts, and so forth — must be withdrawn. Northern Irish Catholics have to be free to elect representatives to Dail Eireann — the Irish Parliament in Dublin.

On the other hand the removal of British rule, British military force and repressive British laws and enactments would be reciprocated by the removal of all threat of a general Irish takeover of Northern Ireland, all threat of a territorial acquisition of the six counties by the twenty-six county Republic. The Protestant Northern Irish must be free to remain British and to elect representatives to the Westminster Parliament.

It is not a matter, the proponents argue, of looking at territories and borders and divisions of land but of considering the people involved — the individual human beings — and letting them decide what allegiance they prefer.

The basic rights of the Catholic and Protestant groups would be protected. All social services would be generously paid for out of a common fund to which not only Britain and Ireland but also the EEC and the United States would make substantial contributions. Given guarantees that the basic rights of members of both communities would be respected, it would not be difficult for the two groups to work out the details — the nuts and bolts — of their post-conflict arrangements.

Proponents of this Irish dimension option point out that schools in the North are already separate but equal: This is one of the few achievements of the last miserable decade. Political arrangements can be made on the same basis, with the local people concerned making all the decisions, as they do in the educational sphere.

So runs one proposal for resolving the conflict.

Any workable solution will need elaborate economic planning backed by substantial financing. Britain, the United States and the EEC countries have an interest in helping provide a stable, employment-oriented economy, designed to improve the lot of Protestants as well as Catholics: a rising tide to lift all Northern Ireland boats . . . Here, perhaps more than anywhere in the Western world, generous funding guaranteed over a period of ten years or more is needed. There are British politicians and people in the British Foreign Office who realize that a non-NATO, wholly neutral Ireland, a kind of Switzerland in the North Atlantic, would be not merely tolerable but of benefit to the West.

Whatever the solution, neither a blundering British government nor British-school theorists nor idealist politicians in the South can dictate it. A solution will ultimately have to be hammered out between the domestic antagonists, each putting forth their own bitter requirements to be forged finally in a common furnace of hard negotiation.

(Below) Under the old politics: the funeral of hunger striker Joe McDonnell on 10 July 1981. Joseph McDonnell rests his head on his father's coffin, while behind the boy stand his weeping sister Bernadette and their mother Goretti, McDonnell's widow, flanked by an IRA guard of honour.

The American civil rights situation, which in so many ways resembled the Northern Ireland quarrel, was initially resolved with the aid of a major shift in the balance of police forces. And the solution applied in the United States conflict demonstrated an important principle: There is a crucial distinction between behaviour and prejudice. Oliver Cromwell was a scourge of Catholic Ireland and no hero to Irish Protestants. But he knew this distinction: "The state in choosing men to serve takes no notice of their opinions. If they be willing faithfully to serve . . . that satisfies."

In the United States of the sixties, radical civil rights legislation was passed.

The courts spoke, and the new law began to make its impact on society. The dominant group in the American South — white Protestant planters primarily — learned no love for the underdog group, the blacks, from these new laws and these court decisions.

But they — and this included their police — felt constrained to go along. Reluctantly they ceded the rights and privileges the law and the courts had said belonged to blacks. The behaviour of the dominant group changed. Their prejudices might take a century to change.

Discussions of the Northern Ireland conflict have been interminably and almost exclusively focused on feelings. But the ending of the conflict is dependent only on the participants' change of behaviour.

The endless taking of the temperature of hatred and anger, the measuring of warmth and coldness, has little to do with the real problem of delivering a "proper politics" based on justice — a politics in which violence would not be necessary because the human needs of each group would be met.

Under the old politics: RUC men carry the coffin (above) of Constable Paul Hamilton from Crescent Church, Belfast, on 1 November 1982. Hamilton, married only a few weeks, had been killed on 27 October in a massive IRA landmine explosion near Lurgan, Co. Armagh. (Right) Eleanor McKerr, wife of an Armagh IRA leader, Gervase McKerr, at a demonstration outside Cardinal O'Fiaich's residence in Armagh City during a meeting with British Catholic bishops on 5 January 1983. Her unarmed husband had been gunned down in November 1982 by a British Army-trained specialist RUC unit (code designation E 48) operating under illegal orders to shoot to kill Catholic para-military suspects. These were among the hundred or so political killings that occurred during the eleventh year of British Direct Rule in Northern Ireland.

R.U.C.
MURDERED
MY
HUSBAND
GERVASE
SEAN BURNS
MICHAEL TIGHE
SEAMUS GREW
RODDY

(Left) Bernadette Devlin McAliskey and an RUC officer in confrontation near Armagh prison in December 1980 during the first major hunger strike.

13
Needs Versus Fantasies

IT IS OBVIOUS that the Bible-thumpers have contributed heavily to the creation of the conflict in Northern Ireland. Virtually all analysts agree that while sectarian feelings are not the central issue they have been a factor. There's been plenty of bad news in the last fifteen years. The good news is the gradual undermining of the grounds of bigotry.

Preachers like the Reverend Ian Paisley play politics with human desire, human longing. They tend to invoke God in support of their political refusals. They promote the fantasy of an Orange Eden, free of Irish Catholic taint.

But politics is really only a process of bargaining to meet mundane needs. Needs can be satisfied by politics; but never desire.

Needs have to do with specific obtainable objectives. But desire — and religious desire preeminently — has to do with the infinite, with the unreachable heavens. The Paisleys force politics away from need and toward desire, where demand becomes dangerously irrational, requiring that a government provide what no government can. The result is profound dissatisfaction.

Sectarian unionism tends to sanctify the British union, implying that it is God's Will. But if union with Britain

(Above)   Rural beauty: the Glens of Antrim in the
far northeast of Ireland in 1979.

184

is the Will of God, then it must require religious dedication. To get security — a reasonable demand — the sectarian unionist goes off and creates a religion of loyalism. When it comes to being British, Paisley is like the Catholic who is holier than the Pope.

Most Protestants in the North have come to realize that, while government can respond to the reasonable demands of the people, it cannot deliver on dreams.

Yet Northern Protestant politicans continue to stand on a sectarian platform. There are signs that their own people are beginning to slip away from them. Certainly a great many Protestants are disgusted with the Bible-thumpers and with what they've wrought in Northern Ireland. Middle-class and especially working-class Protestants are aware of how they were used, through half a century of unionist rule, to

(Above) Urban reality: scene in the Grosvenor Road area of Belfast in 1977.

prop up the industrial, commercial and landowning Protestant elite. "They trotted us out," Andy Tyrie says, "to rally and march for them, and said, 'Here is our Protestant pride, who will sort out the enemies of Ulster.' And when they were finished showing us off, the proud crowd, they put us back into our cages." His UDA colleague John McMichael adds this: "Catholics say that under Stormont they were second-class citizens. They weren't. They were third-class citizens. We were the second-class citizens."

Nothern Irish Protestants haven't lost their tribal sense, and most retain some affection for the British crown. But they have become cynical about the preachers and the politicians working hand-in-glove, inflaming ordinary Protestants with sectarian feelings, drumming them into line in order to sustain their own prestige and privilege, wealth and power. What makes many Protestants particularly cynical is that they remember being taught a Christianity of hate. They are not isolated anymore: They know that's not what Christianity is supposed to be. Through recent years modern communications, television and consumerism have been sapping away at the emotional environment that sustained the hatred. Awareness of the global village is having its impact. Bigotry, as a stock, is in decline.

There is, however, another sort of fantasy on sale these days, and the British propaganda apparatus is well organized to market it. Britain is selling two things especially: the idea that its benevolent presence is needed in Ireland (a cold cover-up for its security interest); and the notion of British honour to which, in their dreamier moments, the British themselves still hold tight.

Most people who are concerned about the Northern Ireland problem are aware of Britain's security and strategic interest, despite its being hidden under cover of "commitment." People are less aware that Britain is busy marketing the fantasy that in Ireland it is the honourable party among dishonourable and savage natives.

Their fantasy has its pathological aspects. It was Britain's "honour" that required it to start pretending in 1976 that there was no war or political conflict in Ireland — that it was only a law and order problem — and to try to criminalize prisoners in Long Kesh and Armagh. The British pretence that these political prisoners or prisoners of war were common criminals led directly to the blanket protest against the criminal uniform.

In their attempt to make criminalization stick, British governments created and sustained a brutal prison regime; this led to the dirt protest, and ultimately to the deaths of ten hunger strikers and subsequent violence and killings in 1981.

British honour, as defined by Margaret Thatcher, required

(Above)   Street graffito in Belfast.

> *We had fed the heart*
> *on fantasies,*
> *The heart's grown brutal*
> *from the fare . . .*
>
> *W.B. Yeats*

(Below)   RUC men in Andersontown, Belfast, after shooting incident in 1980.

(Left) A British solider with two RUC men during rioting in the Ardoyne in Belfast after the death in May 1981 of the hunger striker Bobby Sands. At the gunners' feet lie spent plastic bullet cartridges.

(Below) Remains of one of the victims of an INLA bombing being removed from the devastated Droppin' Well Lounge, Ballykelly, Co. Derry, on 6 December 1982. The Droppin' Well was patronized by British soldiers, twelve of whom were among the seventeen killed as a result of the bombing. Sixty-five others were wounded at Ballykelly, many of them very seriously.

that thousands of men be killed and maimed in her Falkland Islands war in 1982.

Will Britain, which professes to have only marginal needs to be satisfied in any solution, play along with efforts to end the Irish conflict, or will its presence remain the prime obstacle? Will the British ever abandon this fantasy about their role? Or will their "honour" — meaning their imperial vanity and their effort to save face — require them to maintain in Northern Ireland, for years to come, an unnatural, ever more institutionalized regime of violence?

What future for Northern Ireland? In Belfast, on 29 December 1982, a ten-year old boy marches down a street off the Falls Road, carrying a toy rifle he'd got for Christmas.